the Writestuff!

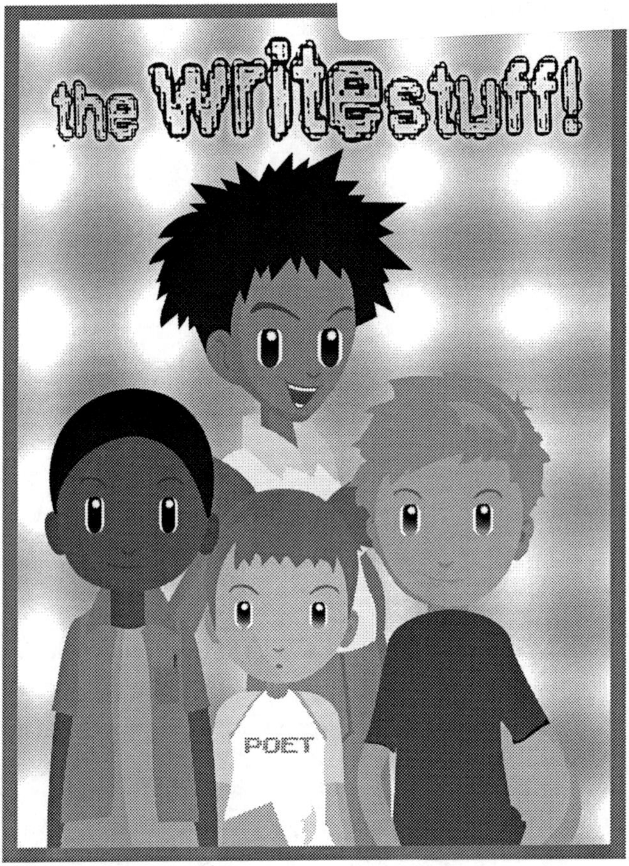

BIRMINGHAM VOL II

Edited by Allison Dowse

First published in Great Britain in 2003 by
YOUNG WRITERS
Remus House,
Coltsfoot Drive,
Peterborough, PE2 9JX
Telephone (01733) 890066

All Rights Reserved

Copyright Contributors 2003

HB ISBN 1 84460 002 5
SB ISBN 1 84460 003 5

FOREWORD

This year, the Young Writers' The Write Stuff! competition proudly presents a showcase of the best poetic talent from over 40,000 up-and-coming writers nationwide.

Young Writers was established in 1991 and we are still successful, even in today's modern world, in promoting and encouraging the reading and writing of poetry.

The thought, effort, imagination and hard work put into each poem impressed us all, and once again, the task of selecting poems was a difficult one, but nevertheless, an enjoyable experience.

We hope you are as pleased as we are with the final selection and that you and your family continue to be entertained with *The Write Stuff! Birmingham Vol II* for many years to come.

Contents

Archbishop Grimshaw RC School
Becky Shepherd	1
Laura Donaghey	2
Claire Pearce	3
Jade Smith	4
Paul Vaughan	5
Sam Booker	6
Parise Fearn	7
Shaun Irvine	8
Christopher Berns	9
Kieran Whillock	10
Sharifa Hunter	11
Danielle O'Shea	12
Laura Price	13
Edward Miller	14
Samantha Rice	15
Gary Walker	16
James Walford	17
Adam McNally	18
Carla Yates	19
Denise Stuart	20
Kershia McLean	21
Maria Watt	22
Natasha Edwards	23
Georgie Maxwell	24
Kira Hewitt	25
Sophie Redmond	26
Leigh O'Connor	27
Ashleigh Henry	28
Kelly Williams	29
Amanda Brady	30
Kelly Short	31

King Edward VI Five Ways School

Rebecca Thomas	32
Kate Oliver	33
Sophie Griffin	34
Brian MacRorie	35
Hannah Elizabeth Baker	36
Imogen Norton	37
Patrick Ellis	38
Rory Nocher	39
Luke Anthony Wallin	40
Daniel Ezughah	41
Christine Hawkes	42
Charlotte Hughes	43
Charlotte Draper	44
Rachel Tuckett	45
Jodie Cartwright	46
Nicholas Birch	47
Paul Tibbetts	48
Balraj Dhami	49
Jed Sharman	50
Benjamin Gray	51
Samuel Strong	52
Sabeel Hussain	53
Yousaf Kharal	54
Ciaran Patrick Kinsella	55
Hurjoht Singh Virdee	56
Owain Prosser	57
Matthew Killeen	58
Philip Harrington	59
Richard Baker	60
Sara Latif	62
George Bate	63
Thomas Bettam	64
Palvir Athwal	65
Alex Walker	66
Tyler Hambleton	67
Jasdeep Birring	68
Ravi Verma	69

	Ravdeep Johal	70
	Ian Cooper	72
	Joshua Phillips	73
	Dawn Grant	74

Kingsbury School

	Natalie Smith	75
	Rebecca Barnes	76
	Marianne Bowler	77
	Ismah Ahmed	78
	Shantel Edwards	79
	Kirsty Bromage	80
	Toni Ann Haines	81
	Martyn Lees	82
	Louise Walker	83
	Ben Howard	84
	Rachel Mason	85
	Toni Smyth	86
	Christopher Wood	87
	Charmaine Banks	88
	Richard Jones	89
	Sarim Sabir	90
	Lisa Pietrzak	91
	Frances Earl	92
	Lauren Hulin	93

Kings Norton Girls' School

	Sophie Turner	94
	Rhiannon Spiers	95
	Hannah Couch	96
	Caroline Williams	97
	Esme Baylis	98
	Louise Ball	99
	Aimee Davis	100
	Kirsty Cooper	101
	Faye Delaney	102
	Laura Jones	103
	Emma Croke	104

Sheryl Pagan	105
Katie Ng	106
Charlotte Langan	107
Holly Hawkings	108
==Emily Hamilton==	==109==
==Faye Lucas==	==110==
Brogan Pearson	111
Sarah Ralph	112
Libby Heath	113
Demi Prescott	114
Samantha Farrell	115
Natasha Greenwood	116
Gemma Harvey	117
Stephanie Murray	118
Kelly Scott	119
Megan Smyth	120
Teri-Louise Grassow	121
Hannah Baker & Amy Walker	122
Anna Harris	123
Jessica Attewell	124
Louise Edgehill & Anna Heel	125
Kimberley Larner	126
Rosie Meredith	127
Amy Wakefield	128
Lyndsey Fellows	129
Nicola Marke	130
Gemma Cashmore	131
Vicky Griffiths	132
==Claire Lambert==	==133==
Charlotte Gillett	134
Anisa Haghdadi	135
Lydia Higgins	136
Emma Gossage	138
Alison Green	139
Alexandra Waldron	140
Kimberley Ohren	141
Laura Preece	142
Victoria Bunting	143

Eleanor Browning	144
Penny Andrea	145
Selina Abercrombie	146
Kirsty Bond	147
Yvonne Forrest	148
Beth Hiscock	149
Rachel Galloway	150
Rebecca Myles	151
Alice Ridgway	152
Kirsty Dodwell	153
Sophie Lawrence	154
Kayleigh Brown Davies	155
Cheryl Priest	156
Hannah Edwards	157
Lauren Wilson	158
Hannah Ward	159
Kerry Louise Welch	160
Charlotte Megan Jordan	161
Harmanpreet Kaur	162
Sira Farooq	163
Sehar Saqib	164
Heidi Edgington	165
Alyshia Ford	166
Tallis Dove	167
Lorraine Davis	168
Sarah Talbot	169
Chloe Louisa Michael	170
Zoë Lonsdale	171
Jennifer Angela Barnes	172
Christina Grant	173

St Paul's School For Girls
Hannah Murphy	174

Selly Oak School
Marcus Williams	175
Craig Clayton	176
Julian Chaggar	177

Kevin Ford	178
Reece Stopp	180
Adam Teeling	181
Luke Bartlett	182
Amy Healy	183
Adam Barnwell	184
Leon Thomas	185
Daniel McNaught	186
Shrikesh Pattni	187

Swanshurst School

Faryal Butt	188

The Poems

NATURE

Nature's pretty,
Nature's cute,
Yellow and green,
Trees of fruit.

Flowers are beautiful,
Daisy and rose,
Until the winter,
When they froze.

Trees are tall,
Full of leaves,
Long thin branches,
That look like keys.

Becky Shepherd (12)
Archbishop Grimshaw RC School

SUMMER

S   un is out
U   mbrellas are in
M om and me are at the beach
M aking sandcastles
E   veryone's happy and they will
R emember this wonderful day.

Laura Donaghey (12)
Archbishop Grimshaw RC School

MY DAD

My dad has got such a big belly,
'cause all he does is eat and watch telly.
He always has the remote control,
'cause he likes to watch Countdown,
I was told.
He always watches Challenge TV,
not like me, I like CITV.
I like to watch Winnie the Pooh,
but he always says that's too
young for you.
My mom goes mad when he eats all our sweets,
so we hide them under our seats.
My dad searches around the house,
but we catch him because he is never as quiet as a mouse.
My dad is such a lazy man,
he is the laziest man I ever met.
My dad plays golf at the weekend,
he likes to play it with his friends.
He is my dad, also my friend,
I wouldn't change him for anyone.

Claire Pearce (12)
Archbishop Grimshaw RC School

AUTUMN

Now the autumn is here again
The whistling leaves down the lane.
Now the autumn is here at last!
The summer has gone way too fast.
Now I know about that cold weather
And all those dirty brown feathers.
The texture of the leaves is very crisp
And the colour of the sky is like grey mist.
The water of the rain trickles down,
When I look out the window, as it makes me frown.
I think that it will rain today,
I like the autumn,
Hip hip hooray!

Jade Smith (12)
Archbishop Grimshaw RC School

MONSTERS

Monsters, monsters everywhere
I *am* trying to hide but they're everywhere
They're in the alleys
They are at the fair
They're in the houses
They're everywhere.

Monsters only come out at night
If you see one
You're sure to get a fright
But make sure you don't hurt them
Because they might want a fight.

Paul Vaughan (12)
Archbishop Grimshaw RC School

BONFIRE NIGHT

Bonfire Night is here again
Sparkling colours and pouring rain
The crackling of the fire and fireworks galore
Going up in the sky and down to the floor.
Kids are running round
Kids fooling about.
Catherine Wheels swirling
Stars spinning round.
Families are coming to see the display
Eating hot dogs
Watching children at play
With rides on the fair, they're all having fun.
Guy Fawkes disappearing
The fire almost gone out
The display is now over
Goodbye everyone!

Sam Booker (12)
Archbishop Grimshaw RC School

HALLOWE'EN

It's the 31st of October.
The day the dead pass over.
All day they can mix with the living.
Things you will see, you will not believe in.
The sky is in darkness.
The moon is in fullness.
The werewolves are howling in chorus.
All this is a start to a scary night ahead.
But everything you meet is sure to be dead.

Parise Fearn (12)
Archbishop Grimshaw RC School

ANGELS

We are made from light
Called into being, we burn
Brighter than the silver-white of hot magnesium
We are the fire of Heaven
Yellow flames and golden ether.

We are from the stars
Spinning beyond the farthest galaxy
In an instant gathered to this point
We shine, we speak our messages
And go back to our brilliance.

Our voices are joy
And the faces fill with joy
Suns do not warm us
Fire does not burn itself.

Only when we fill you with joy
And feel a human's heat
Once, in the brightness of frost
On the hill in the shimmering starlight
We would then be happy.

Shaun Irvine (12)
Archbishop Grimshaw RC School

SPACE

What's it like to be a spaceman?
Will your food be in a can?
What's it like to be a spaceman?
Will you see a satellite and will it be an awesome sight?
It must be good being a spaceman.
I really hope I someday can
Be soaring up among the stars.
There goes Jupiter, Mercury, Mars.
Could that be the Milky Way?
Maybe not, let's just stay.

Christopher Berns (12)
Archbishop Grimshaw RC School

RUGBY

Rugby is the sport I play
I go training every Thursday
In the snow or in the rain
We still go through a lot of pain
When the backs shout to call
They run down the wing with the ball
When the hooker tries to hook
He gets pulled into a lot of muck
When forwards get called into a maul
We always seem to lose the ball
When the ball goes to the prop
The opposition bring him to a stop
When the ball goes to the winger
They tackle him with a stinger.

Kieran Whillock (12)
Archbishop Grimshaw RC School

HALLOW-SCREAM

Hallowe'en is here,
Ghouls and monsters have come out to play,
Graveyard is damp and ready for resurrection,
Pumpkins ripe and ready to glow,
Screams heard from miles and miles on end,
It is spooky tonight,
Money and sweets are being put out,
Take what you want ghouls,
The air is cool,
The moon is full
And it is spooky tonight.

Ah ah ah ah ah ah ah!

Sharifa Hunter (12)
Archbishop Grimshaw RC School

FLASH, FLASH, FLASH

Flash, flash, flash
What about the cash?
You may think they are sparkly,
You may think they are twinkly,
But what about me?

Me, me, me
What about me?
I'm not a money tree,
I work all day,
To feed you and me.

You, you, you
What about you?
What are you going to do?
A bunch of fireworks
Can you see
How selfish you can be
To go off on your own
And hurt yourself?

Oh no!

Danielle O'Shea (12)
Archbishop Grimshaw RC School

THE MURDER ON HALLOWE'EN

There's a man hiding around the corner, dressed from head to toe in
white.
Trying to disguise himself, staying out of sight.
Then, he sees this body, overflowing with life.
He walks over to her, slipping into his pocket an old Japanese knife.
He says, 'Hello dear, what's your name?'
And she says, 'Jenny Brown and I'm shopping for a night on the
town!'
He takes her back to his hotel room, keeping the truth behind his teeth.
He looks for something under the bed and further on beneath.
Five minutes later, he has found his suitcase of stolen cash
And Jenny Brown wonders if he's done something rash?
She starts to get bored and asks if he likes her new locket
And he soon remembers that he put the knife into his pocket.
He stabs her and scarlet drops start to spread.
Then he checks her pulse to check if she's dead.

Laura Price (13)
Archbishop Grimshaw RC School

CHRISTMAS

'Twas the night before Christmas
I was snug in my bed.
I tried to sleep but instead
I stayed awake to see him.
I heard a bump come from the ceiling
And a rumble like a war in Berlin.
I ran down the stairs to see what it was
And saw a big man with lots of presents.

He turned round and smiled at me
And I smiled, as happy, as happy can be.
He stood up and waved at me,
Then shot up the chimney.
I ran to the window to see him fly
And Santa called out, 'Ho, ho, ho! And goodbye.'

Edward Miller (13)
Archbishop Grimshaw RC School

THE LAKE DISTRICT

The Lake District is a beautiful and peaceful place,
All is calm and quiet as the squirrels run in a race.

High in the treetops the birds are singing a song,
Low down in the valley, the serene lake is flowing along.

As the sun is setting in the sky, the moon starts to rise,
Darkness takes over and the light finally dies.

All the mysterious, spooky shadows come out to play,
While all the playful, tired squirrels run away.

As the moonlight shines down on the tranquil lake,
The slimy frogs stay asleep and look quite fake.

Up above in the sky, a few twinkling stars shine,
As the scattered lights glimmer down on the Lake District,
All is fine.

Samantha Rice (14)
Archbishop Grimshaw RC School

THE BEST DAY OF MY LIFE

Blues 3, Villa 0
That's music to my ears.
Blues 3, Villa 0
Left the Villa fans in tears.

Clinton, Clinton Morrison
Scores past Peter Enckleman
Then to put the cherry on the cake
It's Enckleman to make a mistake.

Then up pops Geoff the number nine
Now it's three, we're doing fine
Now all that I have got to say
Is thank you Blues for this great day.

Gary Walker (14)
Archbishop Grimshaw RC School

THE HOUSE THAT HAUNTED

A house that sits upon a hill,
Rumours of a house that kill.
Walls that creak and groan with fright,
A sound that echoes through the night.

Never had I seen before,
But as I ventured to the door,
The birds, they squawk
As I quickly walk,
Up the path of broken stone
The windows creak and the spirits groan.
Children dare not enter here,
Because of their unending fear.

I have travelled to the door,
Something never done before.
In the dark and gloomy mist,
Air as heavy, like a fist.

I tried to turn and walk away,
No, decided to stand and stay.
The house of fear you should evade,
Left alone for one decade.

The windows creak and spirits groan,
This haunted house should be left alone.

James Walford (14)
Archbishop Grimshaw RC School

MY SPECIAL SOMEONE

She is the one thing that makes me feel grand,
I love to be holding her precious hand.
The love and sweetness in her eyes,
Her eyes, as beautiful as the blue skies.

The way the light reflects off her hair,
It makes me want to stop and stare.
When she looks lovingly at me,
It makes me feel happy with glee.

The way my heart beats at twice the rate,
She sees me with love, not in hate.
You do not change, like the weather,
I hope our love will last forever.

Adam McNally (14)
Archbishop Grimshaw RC School

OF MICE AND MEN

A close relationship between two friends, comes to an end with
dramatic guilt,
While their life of the ranch, a dream was built.
A world of unfairness is brought to our eyes,
Being trapped in a place of discrimination and lies.
Lennie and George were like brothers, they were,
When sitting in the bunk, feeling like a minute was a year.
A simple-minded adult, led by an intelligent friend,
They story is completed by the sorrowful end.
The stableman Crooks was the only black man in the place,
He was discriminated against because of the colour of his face.
A sly young lady was Curley's wife,
She was cursed and ignored through most of her life.
Lennie accidentally put the 'jailbait' to death,
He hid in the brush when he heard Curley's angry breath.
The dream was broken and it came to an end
And George had to punish his child-like friend.

Carla Yates (15)
Archbishop Grimshaw RC School

ONE FRIGHTFUL NIGHT

Hallowe'en is a spooky night
With all the themes it brings a fright.
You'll be lucky to catch a sight because
All the souls are gone at first light.
Conjuring all the spirits for witching hour
It's dark and mysterious for its devour
The souls and spirits belong to another world
It's only one night they are conjured for.

Little children pretending to be lost souls and spirits
When the truth is they are far from it.
Hallowe'en is like another land
Trapped away in the times of sand.
The tranquil night becomes less of that
Dark and mysterious, like a black cat.

At witching hour
That's when all the weirdness begins
Witches cackles and different things.
As the moon is out, tension begins to rise
At the sound of werewolves bringing terror to our eyes.

Witching hour is coming
As the knell will begin to sound
13 times it rings
Rekindling evil ghouls.
Hallowe'en comes once a year
Throughout the day, the night is near.
At sunrise the spooks disappear,
Only to wait for that same time next year.

Denise Stuart (14)
Archbishop Grimshaw RC School

THE WEIRDEST THOUGHT

All day and night I think of this thought,
When I was alone one day, this dream was caught,
I would sit on a cloud, watching pigs fly,
When a multicoloured bird passed me by.
Cows could talk and the rain was pink,
The world being weird is what I always think.
Trees would have arms and humans have tails
And the sea would be empty because there's no whales.
But most of all, the weirdest thing,
Is that maybe there's no everlasting thing.

Kershia McLean (14)
Archbishop Grimshaw RC School

THINKING OF YOU

I sit at home and think of you,
Hoping to see you smiling too.
Whenever I am feeling down,
You cheer me up and I do not frown.
I look into your eyes and see,
That you are someone special to me.
Even if you were far away,
I'd wait till I could see you one day.
Your eyes are as blue as the sky,
But you do not notice me, it makes me cry.
I'd love to be with you forever,
We could always stay and be together.

Maria Watt (14)
Archbishop Grimshaw RC School

THE BONFIRE NIGHT BASH

Wrapped up warm, children with glee
all they need is something warm to eat.

Parties start with laughter and welcomes
to all the people who come on November the 5th

Burgers, hot dogs, lots to eat
children moaning about cold feet.
Children having fun with sparklers
watching all the fireworks go.

There's lots of noise all around
different sparks lit from the ground.

Lots of spilt drinks
but adults keep their guard over their beer and wine,
but kids just don't care because it's
Bonfire Night!

Natasha Edwards (12)
Archbishop Grimshaw RC School

I Have A Fear

I have a fear,
A fear very deep,
This kind of fear,
Makes me go weak.
Lying in bed,
Trying to sleep,
Looking at the walls,
Gives me the creeps.
Searching around,
Trying to see,
Little creepy-crawlies,
Looking down on me.
Oh woe is me,
I can see,
A gigantic *spider,*
Spinning his web,
Just for me!
Night after night,
Spider after spider,
Observing creepy-crawlies,
Catching their prey,
Devouring the juices,
Every day.
Come tomorrow,
It maybe done,
If not tomorrow,
Then I'll tell my mom.

Georgie Maxwell (11)
Archbishop Grimshaw RC School

MY FEAR

I have a fear, like everyone else,
About spiders, I'm afraid it's true.
They act so small and brain-dead,
But when you lie asleep at night, there it sits -
Settled next to you.

Its hairy, long and poisonous legs,
Scurry around your garage.
Its huge, round and glowing eyes,
Stare at you as you scream.

Why is a spider so disgusting?
You ask.
I don't know - but its face is like a small Hallowe'en mask.

So if a spider decides to pay you a visit,
Just remember - you're not the only person
Screaming.

Kira Hewitt (11)
Archbishop Grimshaw RC School

Hallowe'en

Tonight's the night I've been waiting for
When trick or treaters come to my door.
All in black, from head to toe
With their little lamps that glow.
As they run around through the night
They knock on their neighbour's door and give them a fright.
The scariest looking of them all
Are the little witches, even though they're small.
The streets are lit up nice and bright
With cut out pumpkins that try to give you a fright.
Hats, capes, brooms and masks
Goodies, money, home at last.

Sophie Redmond (11)
Archbishop Grimshaw RC School

I HATE ALL SPIDERS

I hate all spiders,
The big ones are terrifying,
But the small ones are the worst.

I hate all spiders,
They're black, grey or brown
And hairy all over.

I hate all spiders,
They have long, curly legs
And creep and crawl as fast as a racing car.

I hate all spiders,
Some are venomous and poisonous,
But I've never been near any of those.

I hate all spiders,
They fall in the bath
And can't climb out.

I hate all spiders,
They come inside in the winter
And are usually in with the towels.

I hate all spiders,
I really do!
But the small ones are the worst.

Leigh O'Connor (11)
Archbishop Grimshaw RC School

HALLOWE'EN

H allowe'en is so scary,
A ll the kids are ugly and hairy,
L aughing,
L oudly,
O wls and bats are flying madly,
W itches, ghouls and cats on broomsticks,
E very treater wants his or her treats,
E very parent counts to 10 because . . .
N ext year we'll do it all again.

Ashleigh Henry (11)
Archbishop Grimshaw RC School

HAMSTERS

H amsters are soft, cute and cuddly.
A nd they make me want to hug them.
M y hamster is nice, evil sometimes when it bites, it clings to your fingers.
S illy hamster, it can't choose, it bites his bars and stickers.
T he hamster is mad, it runs into doors, windows, mirrors, the lot.
E vil hamster, it bit my finger, it thought it was funny as well.
'R ats,' I said when it ran away, I thought it had gone to the loo.
S orry poor hamster, I said to myself, it never came back to say bye.
  I lost it for ever, for ever.
  'That poor, poor little hamster,' I sobbed.

Kelly Williams (11)
Archbishop Grimshaw RC School

THROUGH THE EYES OF THE FUTURE

It is the year 3000
And skyscrapers rule the sky,
Everyone is friendly
And no one tells a lie!

Robots are the teachers
And there is no king or queen,
No litter rules the tidy ground,
Which can't affect hygiene.

Flying cars roar through the sky,
All on a summer's day,
People playing in H_2O,
That's posh, I must say!

The houses are tidy
And children do not strop,
Mothers making dinners
And husbands using mops!

The ozone layer's thick and fine,
All due to no pollution,
If today we all loved each other,
There would be no confusion!

Amanda Brady (11)
Archbishop Grimshaw RC School

THE DREAM

I knelt upon my bed one night
and wished upon a star,
I want to be a princess
and live really far.

The star glowed brightly
and blinded my little eyes.
It really took me by surprise
that my life had flashed before my eyes.

I stood there in a gown
and my little golden crown.
I was dancing all around
with my dream.

I knew my dream would come one day
that I would be the Queen.
I was five at the time
but it really did take me by surprise,
that my dream was real.

Kelly Short (11)
Archbishop Grimshaw RC School

EXCUSES

Well, the reason why I haven't got my homework
Is because . . .
. . . Miss, it went for a stroll,
. . . It got ate by a mole.
. . . Well, it ripped in half,
. . . I dropped it in the bath.

. . . Miss, I went to Australia for the weekend,
. . . It was used to give the car a mend.
. . . Well, the dog thought it was a toy,
. . . It got taken by a small boy.

. . . Miss, the cat had kittens on it,
. . . My nan made cakes on it.
. . . Well, it learnt how to fly.
. . . That's . . . er . . . not . . . er . . . a lie!

Rebecca Thomas (11)
King Edward VI Five Ways School

THE DARKEST PATH

All alone on a starless night,
The pale moon up high.
Ever watching, never blinking.
Like wolf on prey,
Where am I? you start thinking.

The tall trees tower above you,
Blocking the moon's silver rays.
You're friends are gone, they're nowhere near,
You twist and turn,
In madness, engulfed by fear.

The snap of a twig makes you flinch,
The drop of a leaf sends you screaming.
Through the swirling mists and twirling fog
Quite clearly you can see,
A pair of lethal, looming eyes of a dog.

You chose the darkest path
And for that you must dearly pay.
For not every path is right, only few can see,
That all routes are wrong in a way,
But this is the most wrong one there can be.

For this is not a path,
To any house or place,
Life is full of screams and shouts, but what is worse, is death.
This is where all paths lead, whether they be good or bad.
So, live life to the full, and enjoy what is left.

Kate Oliver (11)
King Edward VI Five Ways School

THE SMELL!

There's an *eggy* smell under my bed
I don't know what to do,
I've phoned my friends to ask for help
But they don't have a clue.
It smells like something's *died* in there
I hope it's not my *fish,*
'It's probably your old socks,' Mum says,
Oh how I wish, I wish.

The smell is getting on my nerves,
It really reeks down there,
My brother said, 'I've got it now!
It's dirty underwear!'
Dad's on the phone to the police right now,
It's getting really bad!
The crowd outside is getting big
When they've gone, I'll be glad.

The *stench* grows greater every day
I'm scared to look under the bed,
The family's *groaning,* the crowd are *moaning*
There's a buzzing in my head.
They've evacuated us, *yes!*
We even took the cat,
We travelled round the world for a week,
Got bored, then came back.

We've been locked in here with this *awful stink*
There's a pounding in my heart,
I nervously creep under the bed . . .
It's a whopping, huge, big *fart!*

Sophie Griffin (11)
King Edward VI Five Ways School

CARS

Cars with big engines
Cars with small engines
Big off-roaders
Roaring down the mud tracks
Dripping in mud
Splashing through big puddles
As if on a roller coaster.

Or maybe F1 cars
Trying to catch a glimpse of the driver
Whipping around corners
Making marks on the track as they skid
Engines sound like a nuclear bomb on wheels
They tear down the home straight
Into a pit stop they dash
Breaking the world record they dash out.

You may like a BMW
Or a Jag with its sloping bonnet
You may like a classy Mercedes
Maybe you'd like a Ford
With its different classes and styles
You might want a dashing Ferrari
With its speedy engine and classy looks
Or you may not like cars at all.

Brian MacRorie (11)
King Edward VI Five Ways School

THE FAT BOY

One afternoon I said to Mummy,
'How come I've got big fat tummy?'
She said, 'You haven't, darling, why do you think that?'
'The boys and girls poke my tummy and call me fat,'
'They push me around like I'm a toy.'
'Which children are these, darling boy?'
'The boys and girls from school, I don't know which ones,'
'I'm sorry, darling, what can I do?'
'Cover them with your slimy goo.'
'Stop joking around, I can't do that,'
'What else can I do for you?'
'Nothing!'
'They will hurt me and call me a chicken.'
She said to me, 'Stop being a brat,
Go on a diet and lose that fat.'
I went on that diet,
Five weeks it took,
Then one afternoon back from school I said to Mummy,
'Thanks for helping me lose my big fat tummy.'

Hannah Elizabeth Baker (11)
King Edward VI Five Ways School

SEA LIFE

Dolphins they swim all through the day,
They perform in shows for lots of people,
They are always ready to play.

Fish like dolphins, they have tails,
They swim through coral reefs
And are covered in glistening scales.

Crabs scuttle sideways across the sand,
Their claws are very sharp,
They're equally at home in the sea or on land.

Imogen Norton (11)
King Edward VI Five Ways School

ENQUIRING

Impaled upon an eyesight,
Deadened by a glare,
Spiked upon a glance
And speared by a stare,
But as the people watch me,
Their eyes are all aflame,
Like me they've wasted life with nothing after,
And only 'Mister' before their names.
Timid men fall foul of manipulation,
Strong ones never last,
They peer at themselves with pity
And recall their single past,
They say it's just not worth it,
Enquiries about the pub,
Uncles say they're going nowhere,
Almost stuck in the mud,
Marriage is a punishment,
Insist the grandads galore,
They say they'll judge for themselves, thanks,
To be loyal for evermore,
But it's me who's drawn the short straw,
Me who's on the street,
Me who's in the doorway,
Hurt, not help is all I meet.

Patrick Ellis (12)
King Edward VI Five Ways School

THEY CALLED ME CARROTS

They called me Carrots;
Jeered at me for my ginger
Hair and freckled face.

They called him Nigger;
Laughed at his brown complexion
And his braided hair.

We both knew better;
Everybody's bones are white
And our blood is red.

Rory Nocher (11)
King Edward VI Five Ways School

MY BRO IS SOMETHIN' BIG

My big bro is somethin'
somethin' big,
It's hard to believe we're bros
Yeah, we are two peas that
don't match.

My big bro is somethin'
somethin' big,
He sleeps, he works, then
he acts like a baby,
he jumps on me.

I am, on the other hand,
a good boy,
I work hard,
I look smart,
I play hard.

'Luke! Have you done your
homework?'

Luke Anthony Wallin (11)
King Edward VI Five Ways School

MY UNIVERSE

Cold without meaning your
planet drifts in my empty
universe. I felt proud of you
until you created fire once
again. You always find a way.
You will be my death
Brother Earth,

Fighting is not the key
to power. How many
more have to die before
you hear me. You pollute
yourself.

You think it is fun but
slowly but surely you
will destroy yourself.

Daniel Ezughah (11)
King Edward VI Five Ways School

MY DAD

My dad is on a youth kick
He thinks he's really cool;
His fashion's from the 60s
Where Elvis haircuts rule!
I tried to tell him yesterday
That he is out of date
I don't want to be seen with him
Or him to see my mate:
My mate has got some earrings -
Twelve to be precise -
My dad would faint with horror
But his mother thinks it's nice.

Christine Hawkes (12)
King Edward VI Five Ways School

I'M JEALOUS OF MY SISTER

I'm jealous of my sister,
But I don't quite know why,
She bugs me all day long,
And treats me like a fly.

I'm jealous of my sister,
She gets everything she wants,
While I'm sitting here bored,
She's off buying new underpants.

I'm jealous of my sister,
It feels unfair to me,
'It's not fair!' I say to my mum,
'She's treated like royalty!'

Charlotte Hughes (11)
King Edward VI Five Ways School

MY SISTER IS A RABBIT

My sister is a rabbit,
With those big ears she eavesdrops on everything I say,
Then the whole world will know my private life by the very next day.

My sister is a rabbit,
Well it seems that way,
As all she eats every day is carrots, peas and hay.

My sister is a rabbit,
As her ears get bigger by the min,
Her ears are now beginning to hang beneath her chin.

My sister is a rabbit,
Or maybe she is like a rabbit,
Or maybe the rabbit is like her,
Or maybe the rabbit is her . . .

Charlotte Draper (11)
King Edward VI Five Ways School

A Candle Flame

A candle flame is happiness,
Radiantly beaming,
Its cheerful smile gleaming.

A candle flame holds secrets,
Never to be told,
Guarded by a blaze of gold.

A candle flame is hopefulness,
Flickering, burning fire,
A deepest heart's desire.

A candle flame holds memories,
Treasures in the dark,
Each a tiny, precious spark.

A candle flame is peace,
A silent, steady glow,
Unchanged from years ago.

Rachel Tuckett (12)
King Edward VI Five Ways School

MY BLACK CAT

I have a black cat,
He sits in silence all day long,
But there's one strange word
That word is 'song'.
He pauses in his silence,
Takes a breath of fresh air,
And starts melody,
Without one single care.

Then my black cat,
Sings all day long.
There's another strange word.
But that word isn't 'song'.
I say the word, 'Silence,'
I take a breath of fresh air.
He stops his melody,
But he does care.

But one day there was silence,
When I mentioned the word, 'song'.
I think he was asleep,
Or am I possibly wrong?

Jodie Cartwright (11)
King Edward VI Five Ways School

MY FATHER IS A DINOSAUR

My father is a dinosaur,
he's older than time,
his snore is louder than a dinosaur's,
he's bigger than a brontosaurus.

My father is a dinosaur,
he's slower than an old diplodocus,
his teeth are like a T-rex's,
and he's fatter than a diplodocus.

My father is a dinosaur,
he's dumber than a stegosaurus,
his brain is smaller than an iguanodon's thumb,
he's got the sense of an ankylosaur.

Nicholas Birch (11)
King Edward VI Five Ways School

FENCING

Fencing is a good sport,
But you have to be quite tough:
For the swords are quite sharp,
And the blows are rough.

Last time my opponent was good,
Thought he was pretty hard,
But you wait 'til next time,
He'll need a get well card.

I'll chop him up into pieces,
When I get quite bored,
I'll pack him up in a box
And ship him off abroad.

Time to come to real time,
Whoops I've just been caught.
'You've no time for dreaming,
This is the time to be taught.'

Paul Tibbetts (11)
King Edward VI Five Ways School

PARENTS

My parents are not human,
That, I am afraid, has to be said.
I think they may be aliens,
and not Susie and Fred.

They dress as though they are in the 60s,
and please don't ask about their hair.
My mum thinks she is a princess,
and my dad thinks he's Tony Blair.

Why couldn't I have two normal parents
who acted as they should?
And preferably humans,
wouldn't that be good?'

Balraj Dhami (11)
King Edward VI Five Ways School

SOLAR SYSTEM

Our solar system, the Milky Way,
Is many, many light years away,
It consists of nine planets and the sun,
First from the sun is Mercury, then Venus, the Earth and Mars,
Next in line comes Jupiter followed by Saturn and Uranus,
Last of all come Neptune and Pluto
And somewhere in there there's the moon.
So there you have it all written down, our solar system,
The Milky Way.

Jed Sharman (11)
King Edward VI Five Ways School

THE ORCHESTRA

The boom of the drums,
An earthquake through the quiet day,
The trump of the trumpet,
A foghorn at sea.

The twinkle of the flute
A star at night,
The crash of a tambourine,
A break in the orchestra's *silence*.

Benjamin Gray (11)
King Edward VI Five Ways School

THE OLD FOOTBALL BOOT

I have an old football boot,
with its laces all ripped and torn.
I've had this boot for ages,
maybe even before I was born.
The leather is all hanging off,
like paint peeling off a wall.
I wonder if it has ever got tired
of kicking a ball?

Samuel Strong (11)
King Edward VI Five Ways School

CRICKET FROM A BATSMAN'S POINT OF VIEW

Cricket is the name,
hitting fours and sixes is the aim.
Smash the ball for a leg-glance,
hook it if the ball's got a huge bounce.
Take a step forward and hit a four,
get some runs to make your runs go more and more.
If you get caught, it's all over,
but if they miss it will go through cover.
Sometimes you're out and the other team's ahead,
or you'll be lucky and it will go green instead of red.
If you're last, it all depends on you,
make a run and your dreams may come true.

Sabeel Hussain (11)
King Edward VI Five Ways School

FOOTBALL

The day of the big match,
Man U vs Villa.
Here comes a shot from Keane,
what a killer.

Wright sticks his foot out,
Vassell misses.
Enckleman takes a dive,
but the mud he kisses.

The ref blows his whistle,
Ferguson punches air.
The fans cry out,
while Taylor walks away in despair.

Yousaf Kharal (11)
King Edward VI Five Ways School

MY TV IS GOING CRAZY

My TV is going crazy,
I think it's going to explode,
Making funny noises,
Not doing as it's told,
Pieces are falling off it,
The picture's black and white,
What am I going to do?
It's giving me a fright,
All these things happen, whatever channel I choose,
Am I going crazy or is it just the news?

Ciaran Patrick Kinsella (11)
King Edward VI Five Ways School

AFTER DEATH

Do you know what happens after death?
Well, you'll go to Hell.

Yes, to the gushing shores of Hell,
With scorching hot lava
And the killing monster shangrell,
Who'll eat you one by one.

It'll be as hot as the sun
And you'll obviously remember
How times used to be fun,
When you weren't bashing me around.

You'll be sorry for the times
You threw me down the stairs
And the amount of limes
You squirted in my eyes.

Oh yes, big brother,
You'll surely be going to Hell.

Hurjoht Singh Virdee
King Edward VI Five Ways School

NATURE

N atural disasters added to by man instil fear, chaos and panic.
A nimals driven from their habitats by man's *greed*.
T ime for us all to stand still and take stock.
U nabated, the destruction and interference with out natural world continues.
R eap the world's *diminishing* harvests of the earth and sea; if only let be.
E arthquakes and all manner of natural forces though we still have to face.

Owain Prosser (12)
King Edward VI Five Ways School

SCOUT

There's been a new arrival in the Killeen household,
Who fits on the palm of my hand.
He insists on misbehaving,
Because he's only 8 weeks old.

His hair is as black as my school shoes
And fluffy like candyfloss,
His eyes stand out like specks of fire,
Making him impossible to lose.

He's parked himself on my arm,
So it's difficult for me to write,
So please excuse this mess
As he's asleep and looks so calm.

Many fingers have been bitten
And several wires gnawed
By this cheeky little animal,
Whose name is Scout, the kitten.

Matthew Killeen (13)
King Edward VI Five Ways School

STORM

The great waves crashed against the huge hull,
The high winds ripped apart the sails,
The boat shivered against the pounding rain,
The storm had come!

The rain lashed out at the crew,
As if trying to take revenge for something they had done,
They lay, freezing on the deck,
The storm had come!

Turning its attention, the wind ripped at the cliff standing tall,
The rain pierced the rock and water seeped through,
The waves pounded away at the stone, not letting up,
The storm had come!

The ship began to sink,
The lighthouse cried out its warning,
The wind and rain subsided,
The storm had won!

Philip Harrington (12)
King Edward VI Five Ways School

Blizzard

Our house had been on a white sea all night,
The trees and plants covered in snow,
Animals clung together in the shelter, trying to keep warm.

It became day, the world shone white,
The world itself a white sheet,
The flakes that were falling, keen blades
Glinting in the sun, waiting for a battle.

I went outside, seeking food,
I looked up, then I looked down quickly,
You could see grey clouds through snow,
Forever throwing flakes in the Earth's face.

The wind whipped my face,
Stinging and numbing,
The only sound, the howling of the wind,
The snow deadening all other life.

My stomach empty, the weather unbearable,
I felt sick at what nature was doing to me,
The snow caused birds to tumble to the ground,
I found a den of deer, frozen, dead.

I struggled back to my house,
Desperate to get there before I froze,
When I entered my house, I looked back,
My footprints had disappeared. Was I ever there?

Everywhere, animals lying, covered by snow,
The whole world ready to fall to the floor,
In my house, I grip myself, waiting for food,
Trying to keep my mind off the need for warmth.

People were leaning against the wind and snow,
Falling to the floor of white,
You would think the world was about to *end!*

Richard Baker (12)
King Edward VI Five Ways School

THE FORCES OF NATURE

N ature has many bizarre ways,
    Such as droughts or raining for many days.
A hurricane force, when hit the shore,
    Creates havoc, destruction and more.
T orrential rain and flooding rivers,
    Crops destroyed and animal shivers.
U nexpected tidal waves in calm seas,
    That flood villages and destroy trees.
R ocks, lava, hot and red,
    Erupt from a volcano's head.
E arthquakes and tremors shatter the land,
    Like paper being crumpled in your hand.

Sara Latif (12)
King Edward VI Five Ways School

NATURE

Nature is everything,
The leaves that fall in autumn,
The darling buds of May,
The soft snow of the winter
And the sunshine of the day.

Nature is everything,
The eruption of destruction,
As a volcano unleashes Hell,
The explosion and demolition,
Of your weakly shell.

Nature can be melancholy,
But it also can be mad,
You cannot tell which way it will turn,
But when it's angry, you're not glad.

George Bate (12)
King Edward VI Five Ways School

THE STURDY SHACK

The forceful winds battered against a wooden shack,
Standing alone in a field of emptiness.
The rain poured and the wind howled,
But the shack stood still.
The storm's relentless efforts carried on throughout the night.
As morning came the sky transformed to a sheet of blue.
And as for the shack,
Well that still stands there too.

Thomas Bettam (13)
King Edward VI Five Ways School

THE SUN

The sun is like a great ball of fire,
Ready to burn anyone or anything that doubts it.
How many questions can you ask?
Hundreds, millions,
Too many,
It confuses the brain.

The sun has the power,
Full of gases,
It floats into the sky,
Lighting the universe,
Glowing like the Devil in disguise.

The sun is older than anyone can remember,
Yet it is still full of energy,
It looks so much bigger than the stars,
How can it be that it is so much smaller?

The sun has consumed many items,
Many foolish souls.
At first you hear them screaming,
The sun feeds on it.
Then it consumes them.

Silence!

Palvir Athwal (12)
King Edward VI Five Ways School

THE CORRUPTER

Boisterous and wild,
Never to be tamed,
Nobody is safe,
Nobody.

We first see this mischief
As a twister of the sea.
What shall we do? What can we do?
The storm is raging, flee! Flee!

Incinerating the woodland.
Fire! Fire!
Like a free spirit,
It begins to inspire.

Destroys power lines,
Watch out!
Carrying the burden of uprooted earth,
Wind gives out a shout,

'Silence!'

Boisterous and wild,
Never to be tamed,
This dancing destruction
Now haunts another world.

Nobody is safe,
Nobody.

Alex Walker (12)
King Edward VI Five Ways School

THE SKY

The sky seems endless
On top of the clouds in a plane, I feel lifted, on top of the world.
Is it cotton wool? A sheep's fleece?
What is the white above us?
Thunder, rain, hail, snow, this is where it all comes from, as if it is all falling out of the sky;
After the rain, as the clouds clear, all that's left is naked blueness.

The sun comes out, making its presence clear.
It passes overhead, I feel the heat on my shoulders.
As quickly as it comes, it goes, performing a show in the sky.
Red, orange, pink and yellow.

As night draws on it is calm and *cold*. The stars glimmer in the darkness.

Hail beats down in the dark, black sky.
Dark no more, white forks begin crashing down.

It lasts most of the night but as morning comes it all lights up, wet and *new*.

The sky is *endless*.

Tyler Hambleton (12)
King Edward VI Five Ways School

THE CYCLE

It all begins with the birth of new life.
The sun is slowly peeping,
The daffodils growing
And the fields are blooming.

From the cool and breezy days
The sun emerges whole and radiant,
With children laughing
And the birds singing.
Longer days and shorter nights,
The holidays are coming and people are full of might.

The gloom sets back in.
Once again, the rain starts pouring,
The stars are shimmering
And the trees are turning brown all over again.

The sun is hiding but the clouds are fighting,
The snowflakes are descending from Heaven
As the children are singing.
The trees and houses are glistening.

A year has passed all over again and
The cycle begins yet again.

Jasdeep Birring (12)
King Edward VI Five Ways School

THE BEACH

The morning sky is so blue,
The sun shines through,
So peaceful and so very hot,
So much space to walk a lot.

Lying down at midday.
To relax and get a tan,
The children play in the sea,
The adults get buried in the sand.

Splish, splash! Go the waves,
It is night,
The moon is full,
And not a person in sight.

Ravi Verma (12)
King Edward VI Five Ways School

What Comes After Death

After life there is a death,
But what is it like?

Do we go to a Heaven,
Or a Hell?

Does it depend on our life events,
Or is it just an examination?

Are we reincarnated,
And do we become bugs?

Or do we stay with God,
And learn the mysteries of the universe?

Do we become ghosts,
And terrorise people?

Or do we choose
What we become?

Are we able to come back to life,
And become zombies?

Or do we get jobs,
And help out in Heaven?

In Hell are we sentenced to slavery
By a red man with horns and a staff?

Or do we become angels,
And guide people through their lives?

Are we erased
From existence?

Or are we introduced
To happiness and joy?

So can you tell me what happens after death,
Pleeeaaase!

Ravdeep Johal (12)
King Edward VI Five Ways School

NATURE IS...

Nature is:

Wonderful...	but	terrible,
Calming...	yet	devastating,
Unsurprising...	yet	amazing,
Beautiful...	but	horrendously ugly,
Our best memories...	and	our worst,
The bringer of life...	and	the cause of death,
The weakest force...	and	the strongest force.

Nature is what nature can be,

Is nature everything... or is nature nothing?

Ian Cooper
King Edward VI Five Ways School

Rumble, Rumble... Stop

People round the area,
Wake up to find their bedroom.
Clocks telling them it's midnight.
What woke them up?
They didn't find their normal bedrooms,
But their bedroom's shaking,
Bumping,
Wobbling.
What's happening?
It's an earthquake!

It stops.

Nothing left but the memories
And some broken chimney pots.

It was only small but it was the same,
The same as what takes two minutes,
To destroy a city or two
And leave it in total devastation.

Joshua Phillips (12)
King Edward VI Five Ways School

SNOWSTORM

S now, glorious snow,
   how happy we are to see such a shy old friend.
N ine o'clock, the clock strikes, the bell goes,
   we all line up, freezing and inquisitive.
O verwhelmed with joy to see such a sight,
   as we all turn to see the light.
W ho on earth could've thought this would happen,
   as we gaze admirably into the blank sky.
S earching for clues,
   who, where and why.
T rench as we do, through the storm at leisure,
   as if below us, there's buried treasure.
O pen-mouthed, wide-eyed and hearts pounding,
   all emotions mixed together.
R olls of snow are flung around,
   as more of the horrid stuff is made.
M ud and dirt, slushy on the curbs,
   goodbye snow, hope to see you again soon!

Dawn Grant (12)
King Edward VI Five Ways School

MY MISTAKE

A funny feeling lies deep inside me,
I'm pretty certain I know what it is,
The feeling of uncertainty, the feeling of terror and dread,
I feel as if I'm drowning in this ocean they call a dress.
It feels as if my heart is being trespassed,
It feels as if my freedom is going to be taken away,
It feels as if I've sinned and been made to pay.
My heart is telling me not to do this,
My brain seems to think differently though,
I have to do this now, there's no backing out,
'I'm walking down the aisle,' my heart's desperate to shout.
I stand in front of him and force a smile,
This is a day to be loved and celebrated,
But why does it feel I just walked the Green Mile?
The vows are said, I swallow hard and loud,
The rings are exchanged, this is where I should feel proud,
But I don't have that feeling, I'm already regretting this,
But it's too late, it's already been sealed with that final kiss.

Natalie Smith (14)
Kingsbury School

BIRTHDAY

A rush of excitement,
A thrill inside,
This day is finally here,
Another year older, another year wiser
Oor so they say.

I can't believe it's really here,
Feeling older by the second.
It seems that only yesterday I was starting school,
Now soon I will be leaving school forever.

Waking up really early,
Running down the stairs,
I'm intrigued by what will await me,
Will it be good, or will it be bad?
I'm never sure these days.

Ripping open the shiny paper,
Of which there are many colours,
Presents of different shapes and sizes
Fill the floor of the room,
All these presents just for me. Wow, that's good.

Now all the presents are opened,
Only a few hours left,
Till my friends come around
And we can go out
And paint the town red!

Rebecca Barnes (15)
Kingsbury School

MY HEATED HOME

When I get up
I am safe
I am dry
I am warm
In my heated home.
I put on clean clothes
And eat fresh food
There is enough clean water
In my heated home.
The bus takes me to school
No need to walk for miles
To get the best education
There will be jobs for me
As I grow older.
I am safe
I am dry
I am warm
In my heated home.
When I am hungry
There is food in the cupboard
When fashion changes
I can buy new clothes
When I am thirsty
I have a choice
Of fizzy pop
Or fruit juice.
I am safe
I am dry
I am warm
In my heated home.

Marianne Bowler (14)
Kingsbury School

CHRISTMAS DAY

Christmas Day is finally here,
A day full of Christmas cheer.
A day full of fun and laughter,
I don't want to go back to normal after.

As I run down the stairs
And I wonder what awaits me there.
Will I be happy or will I be sad,
Will it be good or will it be bad?

The excitement rushes through me,
As I wonder what my gift could be.
Christmas Day is finally here,
A day full of Christmas cheer.

Ismah Ahmed (14)
Kingsbury School

CHANGING OF CELEBRATIONS

Spring
Glorious green leaves
Born of naked trees
Starved of sunlight for four months
Touched by the sun's rays
Beautifully green once more.

Summer
Sunburnt noses
Budding roses
The world awash with warmth
Holidays taken
Memories made
Just before the summer fades.

Autumn
Leaves fall from boughs
Frosts call on houses
Bright, icy skies
And bitter cold winds
When the trees are finally bare
Autumn's no longer there.

Winter
Sledges, snowmen
Adults become kids again
Snowballs fly
Excitement mounts
Then March arrives
And with it brings
The coming of another spring.

Shantel Edwards (14)
Kingsbury School

LOVE

Butterflies in the stomach,
A single touch,
A caring smile
That means so much.

A single gaze,
Just one small look,
To take your heart
That's all it took.

You share the laughter,
You share the tears
You've had so much happiness
Over the years.

You've kept cool in the warmth,
Kept warm in the cold,
Now you really are ready
To tell the whole world.

You feel like you're flying,
Even though you're not a dove.
It really is a great thing,
To celebrate love.

Kirsty Bromage (14)
Kingsbury School

DOGS

Dogs,
dogs are sometimes tall
and sometimes small,
they lie on beds and at the top of stairs
and when you step over them they move
they lie anywhere.
Dogs can be fun
when they run and run,
when they play catch in the sun
but dogs are a pain
when they need a walk
and it's about to rain.
Dogs need feeding
sometimes it feels like just another chore
but dogs need food for sure.

Toni Ann Haines (15)
Kingsbury School

Mission Accomplished

Creeping up to the chain-link fence,
Camouflaged into the forest.
Clips the links to make a hole,
Eight men slowly go through,
One by one and set up in a cover position for the others.

They move through the darkness,
Hiding in the shadows when the enemy comes near,
They move towards a storage building,
Keeping low and pepper potting towards it.

Four men reach the door, one begins to pick the lock,
The other men in the squad cover the man as he works,
When the door opens, the demo team move in
Setting explosives on the vehicles.

This squad of secrets and of expert training,
Go unnoticed with their work,
Explosives set, they move throughout the compound,
Setting more in ammunition, weapons and fuel stores.

Going to the HQ building they sneak,
Taking out guards on the roof,
Stealthily killing the men inside,
They steal documents and disks on the enemy.

As quiet as they came,
These eight men leave.
Two hours later, the explosives blow up,
The SAS have struck again.

Martyn Lees (15)
Kingsbury School

SHOULD WE REALLY LAUGH?

Laughter
rings around the room
but it will not penetrate
through my gloom.
Should we really laugh with glee
When I will never see . . .
his charming face
his warming smile?
Should we really laugh with bliss
When I will never experience his kiss . . .
feel his tender touch
and his warm embrace?
Should we really laugh with delight
When the flame in my love's heart won't ignite
will never burn
and never grow?
Laughter
rings around the room
but it will never penetrate
through my gloom.

Louise Walker (14)
Kingsbury School

CELEBRATION

We celebrate a lot of things
By having lots of fun.
Christmas, New Year and birthdays
Even a newborn son.

Celebrations are expensive
Because of the parties after.
People drinking alcohol,
Causing lots of laughter.

Celebrations are an excuse
Because people love to party.
Eating food and drinking booze
And dressing up all tarty.

Ben Howard (14)
Kingsbury School

SHHHH! HE MIGHT BE HERE!

The time is here
For it's Christmas Eve
The lights are on
The choir all sing
The presents are all sitting under the tree
The kids all stare
For tomorrow it will be
Bedtime's here
Everyone's asleep
I can hear footsteps
Shhh!
He might be here.

Rachel Mason (12)
Kingsbury School

It's Time For Hallowe'en

Hallowe'en is a time to be scared,
it makes you stick up your hairs.
Witches who tie you up in stitches,
make you turn out in itches.
Ghosts, they tie you up to the lamp post
while you're eating your toast.
So happy Hallowe'en
the witches can be mean.

Toni Smyth (12)
Kingsbury School

A Spooky Celebration

Very, very late at night
When the vampires are ready to bite
Their fangs are sharp, they leave a mark
But they'll wait till after dark.

Children will come to your door
Asking for a trick or a treat
Give them an apple not a sweet
If they resist show no defeat.

High up in the sky
On a rooftop ready to fly
Always be very aware
So hold on tight to your teddy bear.

Christopher Wood (12)
Kingsbury School

HAPPY HALLOWE'EN!

'Happy Hallowe'en!' is what the witches say,
So they park their brooms in the candy kids bay.

'Happy Hallowe'en!' is what the goblins say in a murmur,
They have spots and boils which make you scream like Tina Turner.

'Happy Hallowe'en!' is what the vampires chant,
They have bats to scare off your pink and purple pants.

'Trick or treat?' is what the children say,
When they get to your door on Hallowe'en day.

The sweets are nice but money is better,
But the man said, 'Bog off, before my monster dog gets ya!'

Charmaine Banks (12)
Kingsbury School

HALLOWE'EN

Ghosts come, ghosts go,
Ghosts come when you don't know.

They watch you when you're awake
They watch you when you're asleep.
They even watch you all week.

After tonight their souls will rest
In a chamber, in a chest.

Richard Jones (13)
Kingsbury School

Eid Mubarak!

Eid Mubarak!
Eid Mubarak!
Wake up in the morning,
Standing up and yawning.

Eid Mubarak!
Eid Mubarak!
We go to pray,
So we can begin the day.

Eid Mubarak!
Eid Mubarak!
We go to relatives' houses,
To meet relatives' spouses.

Sarim Sabir (12)
Kingsbury School

On Hallowe'en

The same night every year,
the same hour every night,
the same minute every hour
on Hallowe'en they come to me.

When I am sleeping in my bed
I see witches, goblins, the living dead.
They dance, they scream, laugh and play
I shout at them to go away.
They don't listen, I close my eyes
but still I hear their frightening cries.

Suddenly the racket stops,
I hear footsteps climbing the stairs,
my mom walks in, turns on the light,
the evil monsters are no longer there.

Lisa Pietrzak (13)
Kingsbury School

IT'S A ...

Congratulations,
Let's celebrate,
Well done, thanks!
I'm proud of you mate.

What was it like?
I'll tell you the tale,
It weren't half painful,
Could you hear me wail?

The midwife said,
Just one last push,
I can't! You can!
The baby's in a rush.

It hurts!
I know, we're nearly done.
Scream for England!
You've got a son!

It's a boy, hooray!
Oh, isn't he sweet
Is he alright?
Cos I am beat.

Look at his face
What shall I call him?
How about ...
Tom, Josh, Joe or Tim?

Here's your son,
Now are you happy?
I've done the hard part
Now you change the nappy!

Frances Earl (13)
Kingsbury School

No One's Noticed!

Awake in the morning, no one's around,
No family or friends, not even a pound,
Get out of bed, walk down the stairs,
Come on, it's my birthday and no one cares.
I know I'm getting older, but only sixteen
Teach me a lesson, but this is just mean.
I want my pressies, cards and a hug
This isn't fair, I feel like a mug.
Family should mean so much to me,
I wouldn't listen, but now I see.
Walk out the house, see my friends
Not a word, life seems to end.
Just, hiya and how do you do?
Not too good thanks, I thought you knew!
Hours passed all alone
Why can't they just pick up the phone?
Walk down the road, come to my nan's
She opens the door, there's nowt in her hands
I get closer and start to cry
No one remembers me, I might as well die.
I'm all upset, she invites me in
My family party I find within.
Surprise!
I'm so happy, as thrilled as can be,
How could I have thought they'd forgotten me!

Lauren Hulin (13)
Kingsbury School

MOON

The moon, that knocks on at an empty house and smiles to a silver lake.
As bright as the sun, the moon shines.
The valuable circle of white, worth more than gold or silver.

The moon is where the lazy sandman sleeps and young angels dance
and where fairies paint rainbows.
From the moon the beautiful face of a woman smiles down to the Earth.
Glittery eyes watch the moon and lips kiss, goodnight my moon.

The moon is God's apple and the Earth is the fruit bowl.
The moon is God's.
The moon is mine.
The moon is yours.
The moon is everyone's to enjoy!

Sophie Turner (12)
Kings Norton Girls' School

GOLD IS...

Gold is the crunchy sand.
Gold is the sun in God's hand.
Gold is my mum's false teeth.
Gold is buried treasure.
Gold is the centre of the Earth.
Gold is the colour of cats' eyes.
Gold is love, deep inside.
Gold is a best friend.
Gold is something real, something special
And something strong.

Rhiannon Spiers (11)
Kings Norton Girls' School

TEACHER CREATURE

There is this creature,
It once was my teacher.
It has an enormous tail,
With invisible nails.
It has sharp, sharp teeth
And smells a lot like beef.
It has a horn on its head
And never ever goes to bed.
It likes to run
And has a lot of fun.
And after all . . .
That creature,
Once was my teacher.

Hannah Couch (11)
Kings Norton Girls' School

CANDY LAND GIRL'S FAVOURITE COLOUR

Let's delve into the world of the candy land girl, who sits
on the sky showering the world with sweets of all kinds.

I asked her one day,
'What's your favourite colour?'
She replied with a sudden scream, 'Blue!'

Blue is . . .
The colour when you look in my eyes,
Bubbles floating through the sky,
School uniform we wear every day,
Sadness, when kids are sick with sweets each day.

Blue is colour no one can doubt.
Blue is . . .
Her teddy she cuddles every night,
Loneliness with the old man sitting in the road
with no sweets to eat,
Her pencil case that keeps her stuff neat.

Blue is a colour, don't mess with it.
Blue is . . .
The slippery ice, watch you don't fall,
Dolphins that glide through the sea,
Silk that feels smooth against her skin,
Soothing like the calmness of the wind.

Blue is her colour, her life and her king.

Caroline Williams (12)
Kings Norton Girls' School

BLUE IS . . .

Blue is for loneliness,
    wishing yourself a Happy Birthday.

Blue is for babies eyes,
    looking into their angelic faces, never wanting to let go.

Blue is for sadness,
    wishing for the world to swallow you up.

Blue is for coldness,
    sitting by the window, watching the rain drip down the window,
    while drowned cats cry at their masters' doorsteps.

Blue is for bubbles,
    floating up into the midnight sky,
    waiting for their doom to pop.

Blue is for water,
    crashing up against the rocks, waiting to shatter into pieces.

Blue is for the world,
    as people walk blissfully unaware of what the world holds for them.

Blue is for people.
    the cold heartedness of their speech.

The world is *blue*.

Esme Baylis (11)
Kings Norton Girls' School

BLUE IS...

Some people see blue as the colour of sadness, coldness and loneliness.
Those people don't see blue as I see it,
I see blue as dolphins jumping through the air
And back into the glistening waves,
I see blue as a baby's soft blue eyes,
I see blue as bubbles softly floating through the air,
Blue is the sky in anyone's paradise,
Blue is my favourite colour,
Blue is what you see when you look into my eyes,
Blue is whatever you want it to be,
Blue is simply the best colour because blue makes everyone feel great!

Louise Ball (12)
Kings Norton Girls' School

POEM OF TRUE WORDS!

I love my friends and family
they mean a lot to me,
I can't live without them
I always think about them.

When I close my eyes at night
They sit there watching me,
Everyone I could see
I wish they were here with me.

Sometimes I can't sleep
Because things are whizzing through my mind,
I draw pictures in my head, what they are all doing
If maybe they have fallen to sleep or just awake like me?

Aimee Davis (12)
Kings Norton Girls' School

A SCHOOL KID'S DREAM

It's Monday morning dull and grey
I get down on my knees and pray;
'Please burn down the school today!'
But down the street, big and proud
My school still stands, what a let down!

First lesson is maths, subtract and divide
I look at the shapes. How long? How wide?
Next is English, William Shakespeare
I think I'm going as mad as King Lear!

Mid-morning break, the news is bad
It's raining hard, no play to be had.

Double science, punishment time
The ultimate sentence or the ultimate crime.

A history lesson was fought and won
The suffragettes, women's liberation,
Abraham Lincoln and emancipation.

Lunchtime, freedom, cool fresh air
A sardine sandwich and a double dare
A cry of the whistle, a ring of the bell
Lunchtime is over, back into Hell!

Straight into geography, not all doom and gloom
America, Australia, an Egyptian tomb
With the comfort and ease without leaving the room.

Finally over, but homework piled high
Pull out the books and begin with a sigh.

Slip into bed
Turn off the light,
'Please God, burn down the school tonight!'

Kirsty Cooper (12)
Kings Norton Girls' School

Rainbow

Blue is . . .
The dolphins jumping up into the air.
The sea with big gushing waves.
The bubbles floating, waiting to be popped.
The sky on a clear, sunny day.

Purple is . . .
The colour that I like the best.
The colour that people bow to.
The colour of independence.
The colour that represents me.

Orange is . . .
The colour of my pencil case.
The colour of the sun.
The colour that should represent jealousy.
The colour of my bed cover.

Red is . . .
The anger that gets out of control.
The love we give to each other.
The cross on the English flag.
The colour of our blood.

There are more colours of the rainbow.
As you probably know.
Yellow, pink and green, but sometimes indigo.

Faye Delaney (11)
Kings Norton Girls' School

WHO IS IT?

He is cruel to everyone he meets,
No buts about winning, he always beats.

He comes out only of a night,
Be careful because he definitely bites.

His face is as white as the cleanest sheet,
So when it's dark, don't roam the street.

Shut your curtains of a night,
Otherwise he will give you a fright.

Fangs as sharp as the blade of a knife,
Easily able to take your life.

All you need is garlic to keep him at bay,
Otherwise it's with your life you pay.

He drinks your blood like a glass of wine,
So be wary don't think things will be fine.

This person is very particular
Who is it . . .
Dracula!

Laura Jones (12)
Kings Norton Girls' School

SORRY!
(Dedicated to Holly Wells and Jessica Chapman and both their families and friends)

Sorry is a strong word it's true
Especially when it comes from the blue
Original it's not
But it may mean a lot
To those who hear the word - *sorry*.

S ympathy I feel for you
O verwrought is what I feel for you and the girls
R egret for what has happened
R emorse that hopefully he is feeling and finally . . .
Y ou ask - why?

Emma Croke (12)
Kings Norton Girls' School

WINTER

Windy days, cold nights,
Icicles hang off the window.
Nice warm fire, white bright lights,
When it's like this, I just want to stay home.
Sometimes you get snowed in
And there is snow up to the windows.
Most kids are happy to miss school,
I'm just happy to stay in bed!

Sheryl Pagan (12)
Kings Norton Girls' School

FEELINGS

Sadness can be very bad
And can cause people pain.
It drives people very mad,
Or even quite insane.

When you're angry,
You want to hit something very floppy.
As if a fire inside is lit,
It makes you feel quite stroppy.

Being happy is the best bit of life,
You can be stupid or very proud.
There's no such thing as wrong or strife,
It's when you laugh out loud!

Katie Ng (12)
Kings Norton Girls' School

I SEE A MONKEY

I see a monkey swinging from tree to tree,
His big, brown eyes stare at me.
Hanging on with his long, furry tail,
Through the trees he gracefully sails.
Eating bananas, all fruits of the wild,
Swinging round, acting like a child.

Charlotte Langan (13)
Kings Norton Girls' School

SNAKES

S is for snake who slither their way away.
N is for night where they creep around silent and deadly,
  not making a sound.
A is for Africa where some of them come from in those hot countries.
K is for knowing where they're going.
E is for extremely dangerous with those deadly bites.
S is for *snakes*.

Holly Hawkings (12)
Kings Norton Girls' School

FRIENDS

Friends chatting at home,
Friends at the end of the phone.
Friends playing lots of games,
Friends in so many ways.

Friends doing our hair,
Friends always being there.
Friends making me laugh and shout,
Friends helping me out.

Going out, staying in,
Playing, swimming, riding.
Wherever you go, whatever you do,
Things are better when friends are with you.

Emily Hamilton (11)
Kings Norton Girls' School

EATING TOO MUCH

Eating too much,
Can touch way too much,
You just can't stop,
Then suddenly you hear a *pop*.

Your tummy has burst from all that food,
Then you hear a whisper telling you
There is some ice cream in the kitchen,
If you don't get that ice cream you're going to die,
But then you think die,
I'll have to have a pie,
Steak and kidney will do me,
I'll go to the chippy.

But your bottom cheeks are wedged
Between the arms of the chair
Oh, I don't care.

Faye Lucas (12)
Kings Norton Girls' School

FRIENDSHIP

F is for friendship
R is for a ring of friendship
I   is for impossible to break friends
E is for eating out together
N is for never parting
D is for decisions, making them together
S is for sharing things together
H is for having fun
I   is for intimate
P is for playing together is fun.

Brogan Pearson (11)
Kings Norton Girls' School

PEOPLE

People are different
People are kind
People help you when you're behind.

People don't mess
People confess
People are everywhere because they're the best.

People are different
People are smart
People are very different apart.

People don't mess
People confess
People are everywhere because they're the best.

People we meet in all the streets
People we see are different in mind
So that . . . people don't mess
People confess
People are everywhere because they're the best.

Some people are large
Some are in charge
Skinny and heavy
Brave and in the grave
But . . . people don't mess
People confess
People are everywhere because everyone's the best.

Sarah Ralph (12)
Kings Norton Girls' School

PARENTS

It's hard to believe that parents were once kids,
When they shout at you for telling a few fibs.
It's all, 'No you don't.'
And, 'No, you won't.'

It's hard to believe that parents were once kids,
When they blow their lids when you eat loudly.
'Get your elbows off the table,
Eat with your mouth closed
You sound like a washing machine.'

Sometimes I stop and think
It's hard to believe that parents were once kids.

Libby Heath (11)
Kings Norton Girls' School

THE FOX

The fox walks slowly all alone
And looks out for his prey
But until he finds his food
He'll be out there all day.

The fox walks slowly all alone
He can't wait to see his mom and dad
He's walking nearer to his home
But he loses his way and becomes very sad.

The fox walks slowly all alone
Through the golden leaves
Lost in the woods, the deep, dark woods
Wandering between the trees.

The fox walks slowly all alone
Out there in the dark
And his beautiful eyes are gleaming
As light as a little spark.

The fox walks slowly all alone
And lets out his great cry
He really desperately needs some food
Or eventually he'll die.

The fox walks slowly all alone
Among the woods, golden brown
He's very hungry, very tired
And suddenly falls to the ground.

Demi Prescott (11)
Kings Norton Girls' School

FRIENDSHIP

Friendship!
The thing about friends,
Is that they never end!

Even though we argue,
That's what friends do!

I thought my friend had lost something,
But now I realise it was me,
So now we are like honey being made by a bee!

The thing about friendship,
Is that the boat never sinks.

Samantha Farrell (11)
Kings Norton Girls' School

WITCHES

Witches make a long, pitched cackle,
Little do they know people are coming to tackle,
Some have a pitch-black cat,
Which is always sleeping on a grey, ragged mat.

'Eye of newt, howl of dog,
The wool of two sheep, a leg of a frog,
This will make the children leap.'

They ride through the night,
They don't like the light,
Witches have a horrible face,
On their brooms they have a race.

Natasha Greenwood (11)
Kings Norton Girls' School

MY CAT!

Cats can be tall, small or thin
Cats can be fat, ugly or slim.

My cat is very small and thin
She's always scrapping in the garbage bin.
She's out all night and in all day
And never ever stays away.

Cats can be tall, small or thin
Cats can be fat, ugly or slim.

My cat can be really cool
But she doesn't like swimming in the paddling pool.
When I get out and I'm all dry
She runs up to me just to say hi.

Cats can be tall, small or thin
Cats can be fat, ugly or slim!

Gemma Harvey (12)
Kings Norton Girls' School

DREAMS!

Dreams are made to come true
Even when you're feeling blue
Just think of one
For it will come true, just for you.

When you're asleep
Don't have a peep
Your dream will come true anyway
But don't try and run away.

Even when you're with your mates
Don't make a mistake
Dreams aren't there to waste
So don't be a disgrace.

Try to remember what dreams say,
In November, come what may.

Stephanie Murray (12)
Kings Norton Girls' School

A Day At The Seaside

The sand and the sea is lovely to me
The sea is as cold as ever, even though we have lovely weather.
The sandcastles I build are really tall,
Taller than the highest beach wall.
The waves in the sea are white and blue
They're that strong they can take you back to the sand,
Where my mom's waving her hand to call me over
My day at the beach is now over.

Kelly Scott (12)
Kings Norton Girls' School

Rails

Up the rails day by day,
Don't come off the rails we pray,
Carrying passengers from stop to stop
And then suddenly there's a *pop!*
The doors are open, whilst we're rolling along,
Phew, what's that pong?
The smell of the sewers as we're going past,
I hope that smell doesn't last!

Megan Smyth (12)
Kings Norton Girls' School

SECRETS

My life is in this tiny book
Every night I take a look
I write down what I did today
I wonder what I'm going to say.

And when I'm old it will be
My whole life of memories
It's like a friend who listens well
My secret's safe, it will never tell.

Teri-Louise Grassow (12)
Kings Norton Girls' School

MY FEELINGS

I have a feeling that's spinning round my heart,
That our love has gone away I feel in my heart.
I know what's right and wrong
And now I don't think we belong.
I can't replace your place or forget your face
So if you talk to me, explain how you feel,
Then we could sort this out
Because our love was a gift we both had
And now we've lost it, I feel painful and sad.

Hannah Baker & Amy Walker (12)
Kings Norton Girls' School

MY ROOM

My room is really messy,
It really is a tip.
If my dad sees it,
You can guarantee he'll flip.

It drives him up the wall,
To think how I can live in it.
If you look on the floor,
You cannot see the colour of my carpet.

My room is very small
And I haven't enough room for everything.
That is why it is messy
And there's not much room for a king.

Anna Harris (12)
Kings Norton Girls' School

MY FAMILY

My name is Jess,
I'm friends with Bess.
I'm sorry to say,
My room's a mess.

My brother is Jon,
He's friends with Ron.
I'm sorry to say,
He has gone.

My mom is Ness,
She is blessed.
I'm sorry to say,
She is a mess.

My dad is Mike,
He has a bike.
I'm sorry to say,
He's gone on a hike.

My brother is Jack,
He has a six-pack.
I'm sorry to say,
He is back.

Jessica Attewell (12)
Kings Norton Girls' School

ROMEO DUNN

R omeo is fit, Romeo is fine
O ther than that Romeo is mine
M ight see him in concert and take it from there
E very time I see him, I have to stare
O h Romeo!

Louise Edgehill (13) & Anna Heel (12)
Kings Norton Girls' School

MY FAMILY

I have a cousin, she lives with me
She used to live by the sea.
As for me my name is Kim
My friends say I'm very slim.

My mom, Elaine
Is sometimes a pain
Kevin is my dad
He is sad.

My brother Daniel is a skater
I'll tell you about him later
My brother Ryan is a Boy Scout
I never see him because he's always out.

Kimberley Larner (12)
Kings Norton Girls' School

AUTUMN

The wind blows softly through the trees,
Shaking the branches and rustling the leaves.
Pad, pad, as the rain touches the ground,
Gently falling without making much sound.
The autumn leaves twist and turn
And inside homes warm fires burn.
The leaves are red, gold, orange and green,
The most colourful leaves you ever have seen.
Splash, splash, as the rain falls harder now,
Drumming the rooftops and hitting the ground.
Whoosh! howls the wind and it shakes the trees
And down fall the delicate autumn leaves.
The sky grows darker and the sun is gone
And the wind and rain go on and on.
We sit inside and think about
Those summer days when the sun is out.
When the rain is no more and the wind doesn't blow,
Sometimes we wish these autumn days would go.
Now the night draws in and the moon is in the sky
And we sit and watch the autumn days go by.

Rosie Meredith (11)
Kings Norton Girls' School

SCHOOL'S OUT!

This is the tale of Billy McTed,
Who kept his thoughts inside his head.
No matter how his teachers tried,
They could not get his thoughts outside.
'For goodness sake now do some work,
Before the head just goes berserk.
OK, we've given you a warning,
Now go, go now, this very morning.'

Off he went, straight to the park,
To meet some mates and have a lark.
The geese came - chased him up a tree,
Not such fun, 'Ouch, my knee.'
He slowly clambered to the ground,
Back on his feet he looked around.
No friends about to have some fun,
Perhaps he'd go back to his mum.

On finding Mum she was not 'cool',
Bandaged him up and back to school.
He was not greeted with a smile,
But sent to the head for immediate trial.
'I've changed, I have, I'm not so bad,
I promise to be a better lad.'

His second chance was soon withdrawn,
When his football boots churned up the lawn.
He was banned from school, sent away,
Never to return, the teachers pray.
So Billy's lesson had not been learned,
He stayed with Mum who was concerned.
He'd paid a price to have some fun,
But was it worth it in the long run?

Amy Wakefield (11)
Kings Norton Girls' School

My Dogs

I take my dogs out for a walk,
But then I step and start to talk
To someone else inside the park.

My dogs start to jump at me,
They want me to look and see
All the dogs that are about.

They want to join them and have some fun,
But I think it's too hot in the sun.

The old dog is very good
And always does what she should.
I know that she'll come back to me
And will not stray or run away.

The young one I cannot trust
And so I must,
Always keep her on her lead,
Then she runs at quite some speed
And up with her I must keep,
Then I go home and get some sleep.

I love my dogs Cassie and Pip.

Lyndsey Fellows (12)
Kings Norton Girls' School

GUESS WHAT

Guess what happened on Thursday night,
it all turned out into a fight,
me on the one side, my sister on the other,
'Stick 'em up else I'll tell Mother.'
'Oooww! You hurt me I'm telling Mom.'
'You'll see!'
'Stop it you two, stop it now!'
'She started it!'
What a terrible row.

Nicola Marke (12)
Kings Norton Girls' School

My New School

I've just started a new big school
and I'm really glad because it's really cool.
There's lots of room and lots of space
but when the bells goes it's a real rat race.
Teachers and children everywhere
but I'm having a great time
so I'm glad to be there!
Usually in schools food's really bad
but this food's great
the queues are mad
there's burger and chips
and pizza as well
when standing in queues
you just can't resist the smell!
As I have only been there a short time
I think I have come
to the end of the rhyme!

Gemma Cashmore (11)
Kings Norton Girls' School

FEAR

My vision of fear is bats and rats,
Footsteps behind me and wild cats,
All alone in a deserted, dark den,
When a long time ago this was filled with cavemen.

Candlelit passages, cold and dreary,
Is everything here, here to deceive me,
Imagine if there was a fire at home,
No one to turn to nowhere to go.

Some people think that they're harmless and tough,
But fear, no one can have enough,
The purpose of a roller coaster is to imitate such a thing,
Is it a great idea to copy the great master, that is fear.

Vicky Griffiths (11)
Kings Norton Girls' School

LES CEVENNES

Les Cevennes is a place of complete serenity,
If a sinner were to visit it,
He would become completely cleansed of sins
And if a tourist did he would not wish to leave.

It's small, yet at the same time big, but it's beautiful.
It's as if God wanted to put His creations on display
In a museum and His museum is Les Cevennes.

Claire Lambert (12)
Kings Norton Girls' School

THE SWAN

The swan, a beautiful creature
Full of mystery and grace
It glides over so swiftly
Across the murky lake
The lake is so ugly
But the swan's beauty
Fills the world
With sunshine and happiness
Like a rose that has just blossomed
Its white body is so delicate
As white and soft as snow
Thank you God
For such a wonderful gift.

Charlotte Gillett (12)
Kings Norton Girls' School

I'll Give You A Bitter Love

For a valentine's gift,
I give you not a rose or a sweet.
I give you a lemon.

A tangy strong taste, like the taste of our everlasting love.
Everlasting? I'm not so sure.
Nothing can last forever.
Not the smell of the roses, not the smell of lemon, not this.
Not us.
Not you.

But like the sunshine, the yellow zest promises hope,
Happiness and beginning.
But as I take the lemon into my wet and sweaty palms I clench it,
Gripping it so hard like when I grip my lover's hand on their dying day.
The forced juice starts to trickle down my fingers,
It hurts, and it stings. I am cut.
It is now that I realise that I am holding your heart.
The blood, the love is being rinsed out of it.
Quickly at first, the rush of lust,
But slower as the love begins to settle.
Until it is dry, empty. Gone.
There is nothing left to give, nothing left to love.
Nothing left to feel and nothing left to remember.
Accept the pungent taste, which will stay on your lips
Like our last kiss, our very last kiss.
Its acidic nature will blind you with tears
And you will cry till it hurts no more.
But it'll never stop, never end. Till the end.

Anisa Haghdadi (12)
Kings Norton Girls' School

A Valentine Gift

Not diamonds, not gold, silver, rubies or pearls,
It's coal I want.
Coal most precious, years spent maturing, waiting to be found,
Just like you and I,
I'm sure you will agree.

As man searches high and low,
Travels far and wide,
To find the one for him,
To make the perfect bride.

Like coal, how it glistens,
Sparkles in the light,
Man who has come,
To take it away, to start another life,
(Man and wife).

Young and full of energy,
Nightlife starts to beckon,
Dress up in our best clothes,
To make a real impression.
Dance to disco rhythms,
Waving, swaying, laughing,
Our breath is swept away.

Coal, how it flickers, crackles, reaches for the sky,
It dances in the night,
Redness glows bright.
Energy so vibrant,
Radiates great heat,
The centre of attention,
Makes your heart skip a beat.

Now can you see,
Why coal is like love?
And so precious to me.
Only ash is left,
Where life was once so full,
But dust to dust,
Is our eulogy of love.

Lydia Higgins (12)
Kings Norton Girls' School

BRACE YOURSELF

Not a rose or a lily,
But a brace,
My love for you is a fixed brace,
Hard, cold and painful,
No matter what you do,
You will never be able to get rid of it,
Stuck in-between two metal plates,
Unable to let go or brush it away.

Ugly and misplaced,
Then you came,
You straightened me out,
You were my brace, my rock,
Now that you've gone,
I'm ugly again,
I need you,
Just like you need me,
You will always be my brace,
No matter what,
I will never let you go,
Not even in death.

Emma Gossage (12)
Kings Norton Girls' School

TOILET ROLL LOVE

Our love is like toilet roll,
We get into a mess and just wipe it all away,
We go through rough and smooth patches,
Like a toilet roll can be rough or smooth,
We flush our mess down the toilet,
We absorb water till we split,
Just like toilet roll,
It tears easy just like our love we used to have,
Our love has gone now,
Faded love down the toilet,
Our love has rolled right away,
There now is only rough, hard, brittle cardboard.

Alison Green (12)
Kings Norton Girls' School

A Valentine's Gift

It's Valentine's Day again.
The time has come to buy gifts,
I don't give you flowers or chocolates
I give you . . . a car, a red car the colour of blood.
It will bring you joy for a week or two
But it will hit you that our love is a fairy tale.
At the beginning it is clean and a fresh start
Soon it will end up old, rusty and battered.
You'll abuse it you'll never treat it well
It will pollute your mind and you will
Get so wrapped up in the luxury of it that you
Won't be able to let go.
When it's dirty you'll wash it away as though
You're washing our love down a big black hole.
You will keep all your secrets hidden from me
And you will never ever let me in.
This Valentine's Day I don't give you flowers or chocolates
I give you a reminder of our love.

Alexandra Waldron (12)
Kings Norton Girls' School

THE LOVELESS LOOFAH

I will not give you a little red rose,
Or a silly heart,
But I will give you a loofah,
A loofah from me to you.
It's like a tiger that scratches you,
That makes you go bright red.
Red in the cheeks,
In the blood, in the heart,
And especially in the head.
When the loofah is worn away,
Teared, torn and dirty,
You brush so very hard,
Trying. Trying to scrub the scar away.
But you can't.
You just make the scar bigger.
It has layers,
Just like you,
But soon they wear away,
They tear away,
They stop . . .
The loofah has gone.
You think
And look at the remains,
Floating bits in the water,
Falling to pieces and floating away,
Watching, watching them sink in the sea.
They cry for help,
Just like you.
So when I send you this loofah,
Think, think of me.
Think of the trouble you've caused me,
Like the ship that sinks in the sea.

Kimberley Ohren (12)
Kings Norton Girls' School

THE CARDBOARD BOX

No flowery box of chocolates, no fluffy stuffed bear,
No, I give you a cardboard box.

A sharp exterior, cold and bare,
Corners sharp and protective,
Protective of what it keeps inside.
A confused mind, a torn-up heart,
A stain that will not wash away.

All of this is kept inside,
Hidden from a world that can't handle the truth.
But like the cardboard box I know that you too must open one day.
Sharp scissors will glide through your brown tape,
Until finally you cannot keep it in any longer.
It rips, it tears, long jagged lines,
A path of no return.

You will fall apart, getting weaker and weaker,
Yet still the scissors will keep cutting,
The hands will keep tearing.
Frantically trying to reach your centre.
But when they find it,
There will be nothing there.

Laura Preece (12)
Kings Norton Girls' School

MY WAY OF LOVE

Not a box of chocolates or even a cute card,
I give you a compass.
Wherever you go it watches you,
No place that you hide,
No place that you run,
It always knows where you are.

Its circle shape shows eternal love.
For however long,
Or however short,
That may be.

There is nowhere to hide,
Nowhere to go,
No one to turn to,
Because you are eternally mine.

The hands on a compass are almost like time,
Moving,
Remember every second counts.

Take this,
Keep it with you,
Because you never know when you will need it.

Victoria Bunting (12)
Kings Norton Girls' School

LOVE IN THE EYES OF AN OLIVE

In the soul of love we see a heart,
Yet I give to you an olive
For you to see and see you back.
The ever-watching eyes of love in an olive
Will watch you wherever you turn.
Carry my olive with you,
Forever.

Love forever witnessing in grief.
Creating sourness inside.
Tears will make your eyes red in pain.
Pain which will never leave you.
Only to be joined with new forms of red.
Red so deep with a name you will fear.
Forever.

Hidden within the outer skin
Of subtle green or mysterious black
And the fearful circle of red
Is a taste sharper than any before.
And soon the sharp sensation of love
Will find you and still the eyes will watch you.
Forever.

Love, in the eyes of an olive
Will always be the same,
However you might to try to change it.
Subtle or mysterious in exterior
But never-ending bitterness inside.
And your pain is the only way to end the grief.
Forever.

Eleanor Browning (13)
Kings Norton Girls' School

SOCK IT TO ME BABY

I do not give a satin heart,
nor a blood red rose,
this Valentine my gift to you, a sock,
you may have seen before.

You didn't realise they were missing, did you?
You didn't see they'd gone.
I stole into your garden
and took them off your line.
In the passionate faith and hope
that one day you'd be mine.

Now you'll never wear them,
but they remain a pair.
I'll keep the other one.
We belong together, till death us do part,
like it or not, it's a soulmate affair.

Worn socks shrink, grow old,
but these are frozen in time.
A perfect flower from your garden,
a rose without a thorn.
They may even outlive you
unless you toe the line.

Penny Andrea (12)
Kings Norton Girls' School

VALENTINE POEM

Not a red rose or a satin heart
I give you an elastic band
Everlasting, was our love supposed to be?
Instead pain and grief stretched it
Stretched and pulled in many a direction
Till we grew further apart

Our love started with a kiss
And grew larger and larger
Till love got the better of us
And tore

Beware of the next elastic band you grab
As you pull and stretch it again
Unexpected as it may be
The pain and grief that you caused to me
Will always be there
And it will haunt you till you understand
Just how I felt on that Christmas Day

Now my yearning heart won't heal
But neither will it rest
Until it gets the satisfaction
Of you feeling what I feel now

I hope you understand what you've done to me
But you'll never understand how much you've hurt me.

Selina Abercrombie (13)
Kings Norton Girls' School

A Pair Of Scissors - Love Poem

Roses are red, violets are blue,
I give you . . . a pair of scissors.
Our relationship was together like a piece of paper,
Smooth, clean, fresh and new,
Then the scissors came and cut it in two
And tore us away from each other.
Take them, go on take them, feel the sharpness of the blades,
They could cut your heart in two.
Look how sharp they are, lethal . . . like love.
They could stab you and there would be no way out of it . . . like love.
Scissors, a pair of scissors.
They could hurt you in many ways, you would try not to get hurt,
But you would and look at yourself, your reflection.
It is wobbly and all over the place . . . like love.
Look at the shape at the top of them,
They could be two wedding rings,
If you want, or can be two hearts
And when you open the scissors apart,
The hearts go from being with each other
And are apart forever . . . like our love.

Kirsty Bond (13)
Kings Norton Girls' School

LOVE

Not a box of chocolates or a red rose,
I give you a piece of paper,
The paper, like love, tears easily
And it's not easy to sew it back together again,
You can tell it all of your secrets,
Like you don't to me
You can recycle it again and again,
For a fresh top,
It should be clean
It can bear the weight of the ink,
But if there is too much,
It will break,
It starts off fresh and white,
But after years goes old, brown and crinkly,
The slightest mistake on the paper,
It's stained forever
And ever,
Just like love,
If let go on a windy, dark night,
It will drift away,
Just like love,
You can screw it up
And throw it away,
It's thin
And you can dump it in any form,
Just like you did,
To our love.

Yvonne Forrest (12)
Kings Norton Girls' School

LOVE IS A LIGHT BULB

A gift from me to you,
I give you a light bulb.
A flash of happiness,
Blinding your eyes.
The filament breaks, breaks in two.
Just like when our relationship breaks.
The brightness of the light,
Like devil's eyes,
Watching, waiting, stalking.
How hot the bulb is,
When it's hanging in the light.
Burning a hole in your heart,
Forgetting how happy we were.
When the light bulb fuses,
The light goes out, darkness.
I don't like being kept in the dark.
Is our relationship over?

Beth Hiscock (12)
Kings Norton Girls' School

Valentine

Nothing fluffy and nothing pink,
I give you a pig's ear.
They can come in shapes of hearts,
To show how I am crazy about you.
I will always be listening to you,
Whether I am with you or not.
Our relationship is hard and tough,
Like the stuck shape of my love.
But the heart is brown and ugly,
If that is how it goes.
It was a living thing,
But now it is dead.
It cannot come and get you,
But its soul can.
Be aware of my gift,
For it forms in many ways.
Its alive colour that it once was,
Is now faded and cracked.
It can never be prepared,
Because it is dead.

Rachel Galloway (12)
Kings Norton Girls' School

MISSING SOMEONE SPECIAL

I'm missing someone special.
Someone gave me a special feeling,
They were my best friends
I felt like I had known them my whole life
I can't stop thinking about them.
There are in my heart, in for good.
When the time came for me to leave,
There was something missing from my heart
I don't know how to describe my feelings.
It was the most powerful thing I have ever felt
That feeling is still there now,
I don't know when it will go,
How long it will stay.
I want to see them again.
Maybe that would cure my pain,
Take away my missing feeling.
I try to think about the good times
And how much fun we had together.
But the feeling just gets worse,
Like I'm going to explode with feelings.
I wish it would go.
I have to see them again.
They made me happier than I ever have been before.
But maybe that loving feeling, someone can only have once.
I hope that is now how it will end for me
I have to see them again
I can't last much longer.
I must see them.

Rebecca Myles (13)
Kings Norton Girls' School

POPPIES

Scarlet shadows in dappled shade,
Golden sunbeams, stretch to touch,
The soft silky feel of their red petals,
Where terror once roamed and trampled
And scarred everything for life,
These silent, peaceful, living things,
Remember those who were lost.

Nobody dares to go there, but
Nothing there can harm,
Only memories of living nightmares,
Lurk around the land.
If once a site of death and screams,
Can be gone within years
And left behind to mark the day,
Flowers, small and bright.

If men can do so much damage,
To each other in one day
And leaving behind a graveyard,
Taking all happiness away.
Scarlet faces look up to the sky,
Swaying in the calm breeze,
Those scarlet faces remember,
A time of everything, but peace.

Alice Ridgway (14)
Kings Norton Girls' School

BONFIRE NIGHT!

Every year on November 5th,
People gather for Bonfire Night.
Children wrap up warm in their hats, scarves and gloves,
Ready for the firework sight.

People chomp on hot dogs and burgers with onions,
Whilst watching the fireworks explode.
Purple and pinks fill the black, autumn sky,
Whilst the bonfire rubbish they load.

Parents call their children to stay close by,
Whilst another Catherine wheel is lit.
Cats and dogs cower at the loud and booming sounds,
Till the firework display is over.

The bonfire is now a huge ball of fire,
Sitting in the middle of the grass.
Yellow, orange, red and a hint of brown,
You can feel the burning heat as you pass.

When the night is finally over
And everyone is totally worn out.
They always remember their fantastic night,
Held on November the 5th.

Kirsty Dodwell (13)
Kings Norton Girls' School

TEENAGE LUST

I hook arms with my friend and we walk down the hall,
Suddenly, in the distance, I see someone tall,
My heart beats fast and my mind goes crazy,
Everything's quiet and my surrounding's hazy.

He's getting closer, I think my heart's going to burst,
It's like a craving hunger, an endless aching thirst,
I wonder if he knows how much I love him,
I wonder if he knows the angels are smiling above him.

Sophie Lawrence (14)
Kings Norton Girls' School

SHATTERED SPOTLIGHT

The mirror shatters but stays together,
Its pieces could fall at any time,
Just like that mirror, my attentions shattered and isn't really mine.

I see everyone looking at me but they don't really care,
I live my life from day to day with nothing really there.

Watching people watching me, just kills me inside,
Because I know that they are waiting for me to subside.

The shattered spotlight shatters me in pieces like a glass,
How long will this go one for? How long can this thing last?

Kayleigh Brown Davies
Kings Norton Girls' School

ALL ABOUT MY FUNKY TEACHER

My teacher is quite small
I can hardly see her face at all.

She sits so sweetly on her chair
her feet are dangling in the air.

Her eyes are brown, her cheeks are red
her hair looks like - she just got out of bed.

Her bright blue boots are seven inches high
she thinks her hair is touching the sky.

She's horrible and mean and she shouts all the time,
gives out D merits for any small crime.

She always acts as though she's cool
she looks like she's in Year Seven, at Kings Norton Girls' School.

She reacts as though she doesn't care
when all the people laugh at her hair.

She falls asleep in class . . . right in the middle of maths.

She wears a tight belt over her shirt
and shows off her short denim skirt.

Not really!
It's punk day for teachers.

She's nice and kind, she doesn't mind
she gives good merits and grades all of the time.

She's clever and smart as could be, and is very nice to me..

She's funny, laughs a lot and she's really kind.

That's the teacher I wouldn't mind.

Cheryl Priest (11)
Kings Norton Girls' School

HEAVEN AND HELL

Hell
Red, crimson, purple and black
Screams of pain as you hear a whip crack.

Fire, darkness, sweat and heat
This is the place where the devils meet.

Depressions, sadness, fear and regret
People with sins they wish they could forget.

Pepper, chilli, curry and spice
The place where there is no such thing as nice.

This is what my mind has to tell
This is my vision
My vision of Hell!

Heaven
White, silver, gold and pink
A place to relax, time to think.

Cherubs, angels and golden gates
A place where love is and no one hates.

Love, peace and unity
A land with no poverty.

Cakes, strawberries and freshly whipped cream
Somewhere where life is just a dream.

Since time began
And as old as the sun
People have looked up above to Heaven.

Hannah Edwards (11)
Kings Norton Girls' School

PLAYGROUND SIGHTING

I'm in the playground, what can I see?
I see many faces staring at me . . .
There's Thomas and Jason and Kelly and Marie
And who is that teacher, who could it be?
With long blonde hair and big blue eyes,
It must be Miss Gellaway but in disguise!
No, no, it's not! It can't be, no way,
For she went to Malta yesterday.
Well, maybe it's Mrs Dave or Miss Hackaway instead,
But they're both at home, ill and in bed,
I wonder who it is, who could it be?
It's getting closer and scaring me!

It's getting closer and closer still . . . and closer . . . and . . .

I shut my eyes, I don't want to see this person,
It taps me on the shoulder.
It feels more like a monster ripping at my skin,
At my legs now and a . . . soft tapping on my shoulder.
I feel two warm, reassuring, recognisable arms go round me,
They squeeze me gently. I open my eyes . . .

Mom . . .

Yes, my mom and my little, annoying sister,
Was she annoying or was I just mean?
Oh well, that's another poem . . .

Lauren Wilson (12)
Kings Norton Girls' School

Too Loud!

There's gabbling in the classroom,
There's gabbling in the hall,
There's gabbling in the playground,
I can't take much more!
If only they were quiet,
I could get some peace,
But this will not come true,
Until they decide to cease!
Finally, they are quiet,
I can get some peace,
Now my dreams have come true,
They have come to a cease!

Hannah Ward (11)
Kings Norton Girls' School

I'VE GOT A DATE WITH AUTUMN!

I've got a date with autumn,
I've got to look my best,
Of all the trees,
My colours should beat the rest.

My colours will spark me up,
All brown, orange and red,
They'll slowly fall down onto your footpath,
Where you will softly tread.

Kerry Louise Welch (11)
Kings Norton Girls' School

THESE ARE A FEW WORDS FOR MY NAN

I loved it when: she gave me a big hug goodbye.
I loved it when: she fumbled with material for comfort and reassurance.
I loved it when: she gave me a big kiss and put her rosy cheek next to mine.
I feel sad when: I see a fridge magnet and think of my nan.
I feel sad when: I see her favourite flowers.
I feel sad when: I hear her name.
I remember the silver shining moon because of the twinkle of her eyes.
I will miss my nan but I will always love her.

Charlotte Megan Jordan (11)
Kings Norton Girls' School

SOMETHING HAS COME AND SOMETHING HAS GONE!

One day I went for a walk,
On clouds as white as chalk.
The higher I went, the more I could see,
Of the marvellous world, which was right below me.
The more I could see, the better I felt,
The sun was shining, about to melt,
Melt what was far down below, a marvellous sight,
The amazing world, so clear and bright.
I could see things, the strangest things,
The face of a baby crying and wailing,
At last I knew something amazing had happened
From the last time I was seen,
A baby was born, a fulfilled dream.
Now I had gone away from everyone I knew,
A baby was born, a baby so new.
This baby I saw crying and bawling,
Was sent a message from an angel calling.
The message was live your life and don't waste a bit,
Because life is precious, every last drop of it!

Harmanpreet Kaur (12)
Kings Norton Girls' School

WINTER MORNING

Winter morning,
cloudy and foggy,
all the leaves are very soggy.
Winter morning,
very chilly,
with all these clothes on, I'm feeling quite silly.
Winter morning,
with all the frost,
the sun is lost.
Winter morning,
the snow has come
I'm outside chewing gum.
Winter morning,
are you listening?
The snow is glistening.

Sira Farooq (11)
Kings Norton Girls' School

THE SEA OF TRANQUILLITY

The sea of tranquillity brings
peace to your soul.
As you sink in the water, all
your sins are wiped away.
Your body is fresh and mind is open.
As you reach the surface, a cloud pops
out of your head. You hear a
voice saying, 'Dream on and on!'
You breathe, and a silky feeling passes by
And you awake to find your greatest
dream in front of your eyes.
As you dream, you are escalated upwards,
higher and higher, till you finally stop.
Once more, this soft feeling passes by,
and you wake up, back in . . .
The mortal world.

Sehar Saqib (11)
Kings Norton Girls' School

UNTITLED

As right as rain
As colourful as a rainbow
As blue as the sky
As fast as a cheetah

As sharp as sharks' teeth
As cosy as a bed
As short as a rubber
As long as the motorway

As yummy as chocolate
As good as drawing
As smooth as a table
As warm as a sun

As cuddly as a teddy
As nice as presents
As lovely as my family
As cold as snow.

Heidi Edgington (12)
Kings Norton Girls' School

LATE DINNER OR NO DINNER!

The bell has gone,
I am five minutes late
I ran to the dinner hall
I could not wait.
The pizza's probably gone hard
The pies have gone stone cold
The fizzy drinks have probably gone all flat,
I don't think I'll be eating that.
I got to the dinner hall
And no one was there,
I started to get freaked out,
Honestly, I swear.
I started to walk around,
But there wasn't a sound.
Is it a dream or is it real?
Oh well, so much for that cold school meal!

Alyshia Ford (11)
Kings Norton Girls' School

CHOCOLATE

There once was a girl, aged 11,
who thought that chocolate came from Heaven.

Our story begins one summer's day,
as the girl from the story went out to play.

She met her uncle who gave her a piece,
of rich, lovely chocolate to his favourite niece.

She was hooked on chocolate from that day to this.
To get a bar of chocolate, there is no trick she'd miss.

For her birthday she got a guinea pig, wrapped in hay.
But she swapped him for a Twix bar the very next day.

She took her dog for a walk as soon as he was awake,
but she sold the poor beast for a Cadbury's Flake!

This went on until the girl was so fat,
when she jumped on her bed, she squashed it flat.

When her parents saw this, they put her in a cab
and sent her off to boot camp to fight off the flab.

The moral of this poem is not to love the bar
so much that you end up the size of a car.

Tallis Dove (11)
Kings Norton Girls' School

CHRISTOPHER JONES

The clock struck nine and everyone sat down,
The teacher said we had to think of a noun.
Christopher Jones opened his drawer
And guess what fell down onto the floor?
Little toy monkeys and spelling tests and paper aeroplanes,
Lots of coloured pencils everywhere,
No wonder anybody could find them anywhere,
Christopher Jones clear up this mess,
Otherwise you will go to the headmistress.

Lorraine Davis (11)
Kings Norton Girls' School

THE POWER OF LOVE

Love is a madness that rages through your heart like a mad beast,
It leaves you confused and light-headed,
It makes you feel young and giggly,
It can be as violent as a volcano one day and quiet as a mouse another,
It leaves a twinkle in your eye that never goes,
How this powerful madness came to be, none of us knows.

Sarah Talbot (12)
Kings Norton Girls' School

SEASONS

Hot, warm, humid days
shows the stifling heat of summer
I miss it very much.

But I don't miss the cold, frosty, rainy days of winter.

The leaves begin to change colour in autumn
and the birds start to sing.

Then the snow starts to fall, it's so bright, fresh and pure,
that's the one thing I like about winter.

Eventually the mornings start to get brighter
and the birds begin to sing.
The sign that spring is once again here.
Out come the daffodils, tulips and bluebells,
just a gentle dome of comfort to remind me,
that summer is coming soon.

Chloe Louisa Michael (11)
Kings Norton Girls' School

FRIENDS!

Some friends have older sisters,
Some friends have dead nans.
Some friends have both of these,
And some, they live with their nan.

Some friends have blue eyes,
Some friends have brown.
Some friends have different colours,
I see them a lot around town.

Some friends have braces,
Some friends have long hair.
Some friends show off their cool looks,
Mostly, they have short hair.

Some friends have Heinz beans,
Some friends have economy.
Some friends are not my friends,
Because they are my enemy.

Zoë Lonsdale (11)
Kings Norton Girls' School

DANGER, DANGER

What danger lurks on the banks,
This amphibian gives no thanks,
To catch him on the river bed
Is easier done than easier said
It shows its jagged teeth in a smile
The danger is a crocodile.

It never gives up without a fight,
A whip of the tail and a nasty bite,
All the animals weak and healthy
Try to avoid his sleek and stealthy
Techniques and moves to catch his bait
This unobedient creature doesn't wait.

Whatever he wants he gets it well
And if he doesn't, he will raise hell
He eats fresh fish and raw meat
The crocodile never admits defeat.

Jennifer Angela Barnes (11)
Kings Norton Girls' School

THE CANDY BEACH

Far, far away there is a place
wrapped up neatly in a strawberry lace.
Gathered with tranquillity and peace
it is the candy beach.

With shimmering sugar sand
covered in sparkling lemonade instead of sea
I walk through the candy pebbles
then sit on one of the marshmallow rocks
gazing at the toffee palm trees, my worries wash away.
I lay down across the gummy shells, gazing at the lollipop sun
and staring up at the candyfloss clouds.
Relaxed and calm I run my fingers through caramel rock pools,
then see chocolate dolphins gliding up from the lemonade sea
and watch the bubbles from the tropical fudge fish.

No worries about anything as you can see
right there in the candy beach of tranquillity.

Christina Grant (11)
Kings Norton Girls' School

TEACHER'S PETS

The rabbit is in the corner, sleeping in the hay,
Rufus the puppy always wants to play.
Carlos the chicken, lays her eggs,
Monty the monkey always begs.

Tiggy the tiger lurks around,
Diggy the dog might be sent to the pound,
Felicity the fish swims in the sink,
Wriggly the worm, well we dyed him pink!

All of this we find very amusing,
But we're sure the animals find it very confusing!

Hannah Murphy (11)
St Paul's School For Girls

THE SUN

The sun, a golden ball shining
upon the Earth giving light
to where it is dark.

It shines upon those who
have not seen the first
but new light.

The sun, golden ball,
it creeps always in space,
master, also lord to all planets.

Fiery hot, burning, brick-red.

Marcus Williams (15)
Selly Oak School

GOING HOME

Hours passed quickly as a beam of light,
As I stood in delight
Watching the tide in and out, in and out,
Listening for seagulls in flight.
Tomorrow I'm in flight, but today I'm in delight.

Craig Clayton (15)
Selly Oak School

HOW TIME FLIES

Hours pass quickly as a locomotive,
As I lie on the soft, brown sand
In the setting sun
Listening to the waves.
The hands on my watch go round like a spinning top.

Julian Chaggar (15)
Selly Oak School

GOODBYE?

One year has passed
How quickly it's gone
But for some people
It's a nightmare
That will never end.

People get up
People go out
Saying goodbye
To lovers on the way.

Why it happened
We will never know
But something happened
That shocked this world.

Help! Help!
Cries people could hear.
Help me! Help me!
What could we do?

People jumped from
Window to window
Jumping to their death
Saying I love you
On the way down.

How horrible it was,
Why did it happen?
Crash! Crash! Crash!
Down it came,
Killing everybody in its way.

Screams could be heard as they came down.
Crash!
It's no longer there.

Everything went quiet, not a sound,
The birds that sang the sweet song
Now sang sorrow.
People who were happy
Were dead or sad.

Step by step,
Bit by bit,
Storm by storm,
Brick by brick,
We shall stay strong.

Kevin Ford (15)
Selly Oak School

POP STAR

There was a pop star named Reece,
He sang lots of songs about peace,
He fell out of bed
And smacked his head,
So his singing career had to cease.

Reece Stopp (11)
Selly Oak School

MY FAMILY TREE

Three nannies and one grandad
(Who argue a lot sometimes.)
One sister, one mum and one dad
(Who lived with me, but now Dad's left
And I am sad.) Two aunts, some uncles,
No stepmothers and no stepfathers are in
The family. All of these relations are very
Nice to me and they are never nasty to me
Because I've been a very, very good boy
To them and if
I smile all the
Time, my
Family will
Be happy
With me.

Adam Teeling (11)
Selly Oak School

THE FISH POEM

Fish are gold, fish are cold,
Fish can glow, fish can blow,
Catfish, fat fish,
Batfish, flatfish,
Fish can swim,
We throw dead fish in the bin.
Fish are green,
Fish sometimes can be mean.

Luke Bartlett (13)
Selly Oak School

PRISON CELLS

P eople get caught for robbing money,
R obbers go to jail for life,
I n prison the guards are strict on the inmates.
S ome of the inmates go to different parts of the jail.
O ne person broke the law,
N aughty people die in prison

C lever people go home for Christmas,
E xcellent!
L ie to the judge and you are guilty.
L eave the prison and go home.
S ome of the noisy teachers should go to prison.

Amy Healy (15)
Selly Oak School

Swimming

S plashing and playing in the water,
W onderful, warm water, waves as well,
I mportant games to play,
M oving out of the way for others,
M arvellous moving through the water,
I ndoor swimming pools are warm,
N oisy running under the water,
G etting wet and then it is the end,
time to get out.

Adam Barnwell (13)
Selly Oak School

FOOTBALL

F riendly game,
O ffside rule,
O pposition are good,
T rick the goalie,
B elt the ball,
A lback scored for Villa,
L auren scored for Arsenal,
L ampard scored for Chelsea.

Leon Thomas (13)
Selly Oak School

FOOTBALL

F riendly game,
O nly played by 11 players,
O pen goal by the goalie,
T hey were playing a good game,
B oots the ball in the ball. Yes!
A t last we are starting to win.
L ong live football!
L iverpool are the best.

Daniel McNaught (13)
Selly Oak School

MY FAMILY TREE

One uncle the same as
my dad, one aunt, very nice,
four brothers, very noisy, two
sisters who really like make-up.
One mother, one father, who is very
funny, just like my mum, and a
grandad who rests a lot. My
four brothers
hold up the
tree that's
my family.

Shrikesh Pattni (11)
Selly Oak School

THE QUEST FOR FREEDOM

I looked to the left,
I looked to the right,
I knew I was being watched by all.
I could not live like this,
It was like being suffocated by the
Tall buildings of New York.
I had been hurt repeatedly by this cruel world.
Seemed like many centuries had gone by,
Yet it had only been thirty years.
I no longer felt suffocated, but in fact
Was in a new world where no one could be bullied easily.
This compassionate world was caring and
Protective of the weak.
I still longed for my homeland, the pearl of Africa,
But knew that I had to move on and live
For the sake of my family.
Ever since, I've known how birds felt
Because I too have had that insight.
The quest for freedom had been fulfilled.
All you people out there who have been in
A similar situation need to do something about it.
Be free and work hard for your freedom.

Faryal Butt (14)
Swanshurst School